MW00677961

HOW *to* DRINK LIKE A

Royal

To Val, Dec 2020

Enjoy Drinking Like a Royal!

Cheers

[signature]

To Val,   Dec 2020

HOW *to* DRINK LIKE A

Royal

ALBERT W. A. SCHMID

RED ⚡ LIGHTNING BOOKS

This book is a publication of

Red Lightning Books
1320 East 10th Street
Bloomington, Indiana 47405 USA

redlightningbooks.com

Manufactured in the United States of America

ISBN 978-1-68435-013-1 (hard cover)
ISBN 978-1-68435-030-8 (Web PDF)

1 2 3 4 5   25 24 23 22 21 20

THIS BOOK IS DEDICATED TO
my godson and cousin,

SPENCER WHEATCROFT.

CONTENTS

ACKNOWLEDGMENTS

I WISH TO THANK MANY people for their contributions and support as I wrote this book:

My wife, Kim, for her love, support, and copyediting.

My sons, Tom and Mike, for inspiring me to always do my best.

My mother, Elizabeth Schmid, for all of her support and advice.

My sisters and brothers, Gretchen, Rachel, Justin, Bennett, Ana, Shane, and John, for their support.

My friend and former student Loreal "the Butcher Babe" Gavin, whose enthusiasm is infectious.

My friend and attorney Scot Duval, for his friendly counsel.

My friend Gary Gruver, mentor mixologist.

My friends Brian and Angie Clute—looking forward to the next trip!

My longtime friend Keith Mellage.

My friend and mentor Lou Mongello, for his advice and support and for giving momentum to my projects and to me.

My momentum accountability partners, Erin King, David Tarnoff, and Scott Cornelius, for their advice, support, and friendship.

The artists who made me laugh, smile, and dance while working on this project: Justin Timberlake, Jimmy Fallon, James Corden, Ellen DeGeneres, Bill Murray, Bill Burr, George Carlin, Etta James, Frank Sinatra, Alicia Keys, Jill Scott, Jay-Z, Dr. Dre, Bruno Mars, Maroon 5, Herb Alpert, Miles Davis, Michael Bublé, Snoop Dogg, Mark Ronson, Stacy Kent, and Greta Van Fleet.

HOW *to* DRINK LIKE A

Royal

ONE

Royal Lexicon

THE FOLLOWING ARE TERMS RELATED to the world of royals and nobles.

Accession The attainment or acquisition of a position of rank or power. The accession of the crown prince or crown princess to the crown is automatic upon the death of the king.

Ampulla and spoon An ampulla is a small round container used to hold holy oil or water for anointing a monarch. The spoon is used to hold the liquid during the anointing ceremony.

Aristocracy The highest class in societies—in many cases, those holding hereditary titles or offices.

Aristocrat A member of the aristocracy.

Armillas Bracelets used in the coronation of a monarch, one for each arm, symbolizing sincerity and wisdom.

Baron The lowest order of most nobilities. Most barons are referred to as *Lord* with the name of their barony listed directly after. For example, Peter Maxwell is the 27th Baron de Ros; as such, he is referred to as Lord de Ros.

Baroness A female member of the lowest order of most nobilities. This can also be a courtesy title afforded to

the consort of a baron. Most baronesses are referred to
as *Lady*.

Baronet A member of the lowest hereditary titled British
order. A baronet is considered a commoner but is able
to use the prefix *Sir*. The courtesy title for the wife of a
baronet is *Lady*.

Barony The domain of a baron.

Blue blood An aristocrat, noble, or member of a socially
prominent family.

Consort The wife or husband of a reigning monarch; also,
the wife or husband of a noble lord or lady.

Count The middle rank of nobility, above a viscount and
below a marquess but usually referring to continental
Europe. It is the equivalent rank of earl. The English
term *county* is a derivative word from *count* and once
referred to a count's or earl's domain.

Countess The female equivalent of a count or earl; also, a
courtesy title afforded to the consort of a count or earl.

County The domain of a count or earl.

Court The extended royal household of a monarchy,
including those who attend to the monarchy.

Courtesy title A title afforded to someone related to a
peer or noble (e.g., a wife, son, or daughter) with the
legal right to the title.

Crown The crown can refer to the headgear that is an
emblem of a monarch or to the legal embodiment of
governance in the realm of the Commonwealth of
Nations.

Crown prince The male heir apparent to the throne in a
royal or imperial monarchy. An example is Haakon,
Crown Prince of Norway. In some monarchies, another
title signifies this status. For example, the Prince of
Wales is the crown prince for the United Kingdom

and the Commonwealth nations. Other examples include Prince of Asturias in Spain, Duke of Brabant in Belgium, and Prince of Orange in the Netherlands.

Crown princess The female equivalent of a crown prince. Examples include Princess Elisabeth, Duchess of Brabant, and Victoria, Crown Princess of Sweden, Duchess of Västergötland. Also, this is a courtesy title for the consort of the crown prince.

Crowned head A king, a queen, or another monarch.

Czar (tsar) An Eastern European title that is equivalent to emperor. Examples include the former rulers of Russia and the rulers of Bulgaria. The last tsar of Bulgaria, Simeon II, was forced to abdicate in 1946 and flee to Spain. He returned in 1996 and would serve as Bulgaria's prime minister from 2001 to 2005.

Czarina The female equivalent of a czar or the courtesy title for the consort to a czar.

Dame The female equivalent of a knight.

Dethronement The removal of a monarch from power.

Dowager A widow whose husband held a title and whose heir has ascended to the title. This helps to reduce confusion between the peer's mother and wife or between the peer and the peer's mother.

Ducal Related to a duke or dukedom.

Duchess The female equivalent of a duke or the courtesy title of the consort to a duke.

Duke (archduke, grand duke) The highest order of noble; above a marquess. A duke is referred to as *Your Grace*. In imperial courts, there existed the rank of archduke. The Grand Duke of Luxemburg is the last grand duke in existence.

Dukedom The title, office, and territory of a duke.

Earl The British equivalent of a count. Most earls are referred to as *Lord*.

Earldom The title, office, and territory of an earl.

Emir A ruler or chief in some Islamic countries.

Emperor A royal ruler of an empire, one who is senior to a king. Historically, an emperor was a "king of kings"; the empire would include kingdoms, and the kings would report to or be subject to the emperor.

Empress A female equivalent of an emperor, ruler of an empire; also, the courtesy title of the consort of an emperor.

Ennoble To give someone a noble title or rank.

Esquire Traditionally, a young nobleman training for knighthood; also, a title for an officer in the service of a king or nobleman.

Hereditary peerage A peerage that can pass from parent to child.

Honourable A courtesy title used by younger sons of earls, viscounts, and barons.

Honours list A list released each New Year and on the king's or queen's birthday bestowing honours (orders, awards, medals, and peerages) on deserving subjects.

Honours system The sovereign is considered the *fount of honour*. The honours system consists of three types of awards to reward service, achievement, and bravery. The awards include honours, decorations, and medals. These can include peerages (both hereditary and life—although for the most part only life peerages are awarded now), knighthood (orders), and medals documenting specific acts.

House Refers to the dynasty or the name of the family ruling. For example, Queen Elizabeth II is a member of the House of Windsor. King Felipe VI of Spain is a member of the House of Bourbon-Anjou.

HH (His [or Her] Highness) A style used by princes and princesses from a cadet line of a royal family and a nonruling prince or princess. Seen as a lower form of address to HSH.

HIH (His [or Her] Imperial Highness) A style used by a prince or princess who is directly descended from an emperor or empress. A higher form of address to HRH.

HI&RH (His [or Her] Imperial and Royal Highness) A style used by a prince or princess who is descended from or married into both a royal and imperial household.

HRH (His [or Her] Royal Highness) A style used by princes and princesses in a royal house. This style is often extended to a prince's consort. Seen as a higher form of address to HSH.

HSH (His [or Her] Serene Highness) A style used by the princes and princesses in the houses of Monaco, Liechtenstein, and Thailand. Seen as a lower form of address to HRH.

King The male monarch of a kingdom. The title *king consort* is used, though rarely, for the husband of a queen regnant.

Kingship The state of being a king.

Knight An honorary title granted to men by a monarch or religious leader.

Lady Usually a courtesy title for the wife of a knight, the wife of a noble, or the daughter of an earl, a marquess, or a duke. In some cases, the title used for a noblewoman in her own right. Also, used for female judges in Britain.

Life peer (life peerage) A peerage created for a specific person that cannot be inherited by the peer's children or descendants.

Lord Title used for three categories of British men male members of the aristocracy, the judiciary, and bishops.

Lord is also a courtesy title of the sons of marquesses and dukes.

Mace A symbol of the monarch's authority usually carried during ceremonies such as a coronation or the opening of parliament.

Maharaja Sanskrit title for a ruler that is equivalent to an emperor, with a literal translation of *great king* or *high king*.

Maharani The female equivalent of maharaja or a courtesy title for the wife of a maharaja.

Majesty (Imperial Majesty) A style used by a ruling or former ruling king or queen and their consort. The addition of *Imperial* is for a ruling or former ruling emperor or empress and their consort.

Marchioness The female equivalent of a marquess and the courtesy title for the wife of a marquess.

Marquess The upper-middle rank of nobility, above an earl (or a count) and below a duke. Usually referred to as *Lord*.

MBE (OBE, CBE, KBE, GBE) The British order of chivalry, the Most Excellent Order of the British Empire, established by George V. There are five levels, in ascending order Member of the Most Excellent Order of the British Empire (MBE), Officer of the Most Excellent Order of the British Empire (OBE), Commander of the Most Excellent Order of the British Empire (CBE), Knight Commander (Dame Commander) of the Most Excellent Order of the British Empire (KBE), and Knight Grand Cross (Dame Grand Cross) of the Most Excellent Order of the British Empire (GBE).

Orb and cross (globus cruciger) Usually part of the crown jewels. The orb is a Christian symbol of authority and symbolizes the monarch holding the world in their hand.

Order of chivalry (order of knighthood) Today, historic orders of knighthood are honorific associations used to honor individuals for great deeds or as a way to build loyalty. Examples include the Most Noble Order of the Garter, the Distinguished Order of the Golden Fleece, the Royal Order of the Seraphim, the Order of the Holy Spirit, and the Order of Leopold.

Palace A royal residence. The home of a monarch or a bishop. This term can also refer to a grand residence of a head of state or dignitary.

Patrician A member of the ruling class. This term can include but is not limited to members of the royal family, noble families, and well-connected and wealthy commoners.

Peer (peer of the realm) A member of the nobility. A peer is high in the social order but not a member of the ruling family.

Prince A male ruler of a country ranked above a duke and below a king. Typically, a prince is a ruler of a country (for example, Albert II, Prince of Monaco, or Hans-Adams II, Prince of Liechtenstein), but a prince can also be the son of a king or emperor (for example, Fumihito, the Crown Prince of Japan, younger son of the emperor emeritus and brother to the current emperor).

Prince consort The husband of a queen. Sometimes the title is formal, as in the case of Prince Albert, Queen Victoria's prince consort, or informal, as in the case of Prince Phillip, Queen Elizabeth's prince consort.

Prince of the blood (prince du sang) A prince of the royal house who is descended from a king but is not a member of the immediate family of the current monarch.

Prince of Wales The crown prince of Great Britain.

Princess The female equivalent of a prince; also, the courtesy title for the wife of a prince.

Princess of Wales The consort of the Prince of Wales. In most cases, this is a formal courtesy title, as in the case of Diana, Princess of Wales. In the case of Camilla, Duchess of Cornwall, this courtesy title is used informally.

Queen The title for a female monarch of a kingdom; also, the courtesy title for the wife of a king.

Queen Mother The mother of a monarch.

Robes Symbols of a monarch's divine nature. This is because robes are usually associated with the clergy.

Scepter A rod held by the monarch as a symbol of a monarch's temporal power as head of state.

Spurs A pointed device secured to a horse rider's boot near the heel that is used to urge the horse to move forward. A monarch is part of the fighting class and is therefore a knight. When spurs are used in a coronation, they are a symbol of knighthood. Today, they are rarely used, as monarchs rarely fight in the field.

Sword(s) A weapon with a long blade used for thrusting or cutting. During a coronation, swords symbolize the monarch's role as commander in chief. Similar to the spurs, the sword represents the monarch's connection to knighthood. Sometimes multiple swords are used, each representing a different aspect of a monarch's power. For example, there might be three separate swords one for mercy, one for justice, and one for state.

Throne A symbol of the seat of power of a monarchy or other ruler, political or religious.

Trumpets Used to announce a monarch during a coronation or when a monarch entered a party.

Viceroy Someone who rules or administers an area, region, or colony in place of the monarch. The term is derived from Latin, meaning *in place of* (*vice*) the *king* (*roy*).

Viscount The lower middle rank of nobility, above a baron and below an earl (or count). Viscounts are usually referred to as *Lord*.

Viscountess The female equivalent of a viscount. The courtesy title for the wife of a count or an earl.

TWO

Drink Like a Royal

THE WORLD IS OBSESSED WITH royals! We watch their every move: where they go, who they date, the cars they drive, their successes, and the mistakes they make. From birth, the very details of their lives are reported to royal-hungry audiences of television, newspapers, and magazines. Royals have very little privacy. To be born royal is to be born an instant celebrity. From the outside looking in, every day is a celebration, and they get invitations to the best parties. Parties with movie stars, rock stars, and other VIPs—not to mention the titles, the privilege, and the fortune—all attract attention and scrutiny. Even in countries that have "thrown off such government," such as the United States, little girls dream of being princesses and little boys dream of being princes or knights. As they grow, there is still a little part of them that would love to believe it could still happen. For a few commoners, like Kate Middleton, Meghan Markle, Grace Kelly, Letizia Ortiz Rocasolano, Daniel Westling, Christopher O'Neill, Máxima Zorreguieta Cerruti, Antony Armstrong-Jones, Mark Phillips, Mette-Marit Høiby, Mary Donaldson, Sophie Rhys-Jones, and Sarah Ferguson, this dream became reality. In some cases, the reality was a fairy tale; in other cases, a nightmare.

The original purpose for royal and noble houses was for the protection of the land and people on the land. They were the fighting class. Those born into modern royalty view their lives as obligated service to those they rule. Very few actually fight, although they almost always serve in the military. This obligation to service helps—at least, according to the good royals—to mobilize people and advance noble causes. An example of a pledge of service came in 1947, when then Princess Elizabeth said during a broadcast to the Commonwealth, "I declare before you all that my whole life, whether it be long or short, shall be devoted to your service and the service of our great imperial family to which we all belong." Five years later, her father, King George VI, would pass away. King George was dead. Long live Queen Elizabeth! She is still serving almost seven decades later.

Of course, part of that service comes with amazing parties. Do you want to party like a royal? Many of the rules that apply to the commoners don't apply to those who are royal—or at least that is the perception. However, there is a clear set of rules that do apply.

RULES FOR DRINKING COCKTAILS LIKE A ROYAL

When the monarch stands, you stand They are, after all, the monarch. But standing is also a good way to welcome people to your table.

No one can eat after the monarch has finished their meal This is a good rule for drinking. Don't order a drink unless the group is ordering a drink.

Public displays of affection (PDAs) are frowned upon Physical affection is great for private moments but not good in public.

Avoid talking about politics or religion Neither is good to speak about when drinking.

The family isn't allowed to sign autographs or take selfies What is uploaded to the internet stays on the internet *forever*! Be careful what you post online while drinking.

The royal family must adhere to a strict dress code A dress code is good for going out to the bars too. Both men and women should be careful what they wear in public. A clean-cut, put-together image is key. Neither cleavage nor chest hair are part of the royal dress code.

Women are expected to sit a certain way Knees are together, and one foot is folded under the other.

Don't use nicknames You may do so, however, if the person says they prefer the nickname.

Know how to converse When introduced to someone, say, "How do you do?" When you leave the table, leave with little fuss and just say, "Excuse me." Whatever you do, don't use the words *toilet* or *pardon*.

Know your limits Don't overconsume alcohol! Remember the press is watching and pictures last forever.

THE HOME BAR

Those who plan to create their own bar at home or who already have a bar might consider checking or double-checking to make sure that they have the following items to maximize their and their guests' experiences.

MENU

Write a menu of the drinks that you feel confident you can make when your friends visit. Make sure these are drinks that you can produce quickly and with little effort so that you don't spend time flipping through books. For example, David A. Embury, the author of *The Fine Art of Mixing Drinks*, which was published in 1948, writes that the average host "can get along very nicely" knowing how to make six good cocktails. He suggests the gin martini, the Manhattan, the old-fashioned, the daiquiri, the sidecar, and the Jack Rose, all of which still work almost fourscore years later. Start small and simple with one drink. Once you have perfected the one, set a goal for five drinks; then expand to ten drinks as you learn them, and set the goal of twenty drinks later. Spend time studying drinks away from the bar so you can expand your menu. A menu will keep you focused and will keep your inventory small and focused too. The more drinks you add to that list, the more inventory you need on hand so you can produce the drinks on that menu.

SETTING THE BAR

Make sure you have the correct equipment for your bar. You might include one or more of each of the following pieces of equipment. Royals are confident and come to each event prepared. Royals' bartenders always have the correct utensils for the occasion.

Bar mat   Bar mats come in assorted sizes and assorted colors, which means you can look for the perfect mat to match your bar or the decor of your home. Bar mats provide a stable, slip-free place to mix drinks. They will also contain spills and protect the surface below the mat.

Barspoon   The barspoon is one of the most important tools of a bartender. Generally, the barspoon is very long—about eleven inches—with a twisted handle, and it has a spoon at one end and a disk at the other. The twisted handle aids the bartender in stirring a drink in a mixing glass. The disk can be used to muddle (press) soft items against the glass and can also be used to float bands of different alcohols in a glass for a classic layered drink.

Blender Every house and bar should have a blender, no matter what you think of blended drinks. There are some drinks that really should be blended. If you are going to use a blender, make sure to use ice that is already crushed: this will add years to the blades and the overall life of the blender. Examples of blended drinks include the margarita, the piña colada, and daiquiris.

Channel knife A channel knife is a small tool that helps the bartender create citrus twists. The blade of the tool cuts perfect twists, both short and long, to garnish drinks.

Citrus squeezer Fresh fruit juice makes a cocktail. The citrus squeezer is a tool that comes in numerous sizes specifically for limes, lemons, and other citrus fruits such as oranges and grapefruit. The tool acts as a lever that closes around the fruit, squeezing the juice out of the fruit.

Corkscrew A good corkscrew is important to have on hand to remove corks and bottle caps from bottles. The twisted "worm" is inserted into the cork to grab the cork for removal.

Ice Ice is a tool as well as part of the drink. Ice helps cool a drink quickly and chill the glass. Ice comes in diverse sizes and shapes. Bartenders should choose the ice size and shape based on the drink being created. Generally, ice comes in three shapes: cubed, crushed, and shaved. Today, there are many choices for molds and cut ice.

Ice scoop Ice should always be scooped into a glass. An ice scoop is a handled scoop that allows the bartender to effortlessly move ice from the ice bin to the mixing glass or to the drinking glass.

Jigger A jigger is a small two-sided hourglass-shaped measuring cup that is used to quickly and accurately measure out various portions of liquor, liqueur, juice, and other liquids to make cocktails. Most common jiggers are 1½ ounces on the large side and 1 ounce or less on the small side.

Julep strainer The julep strainer is a curved plate strainer made from stainless steel that is used to strain drinks from the mixing glass when there is no need for a fine strain.

Knife and cutting board A sharp paring knife should always be part of a properly equipped bar. Knives are used to cut fruit and make garnishes. The cutting board should be small—just large enough to hold a piece of fruit.

Muddler A muddler is a small bat-shaped stick of wood or rod of metal. The muddler is used to crush sugar cubes and citrus fruits so they can be incorporated into the drink.

Napkins Napkins add a little class to the drink and will collect any condensation on the outside of the glass, so it does not damage the surface on which the glass is sitting. The color and design of the napkin can coordinate or contrast the bar.

Pour spout For a professional-looking bar, each bottle should be outfitted with a pour spout. This tool allows the bartender to create a consistent flow of liquid from any bottle. This reliable flow allows the bartender to reduce waste when pouring drinks.

Shaker Bartenders use two distinct types of shakers: the Boston shaker and the cobbler shaker. The Boston shaker comes in two parts: the tin and the mixing glass. If you use a Boston shaker, you will also need to purchase a strainer to hold the ice in the shaker when straining the drink into the glass. The cobbler shaker is a self-contained shaker, tin, and strainer all in one.

Small mesh strainer A small mesh strainer is used to strain out small chips of ice from a drink that is already being strained from a mixing glass or shaker. Sometimes this is referred to as the double strain.

Strainer A drink should always be served over fresh ice, which means a drink that is mixed or shaken should be strained from the mixing glass or shaker into a glass that contains fresh ice. For a drink that is served straight up, the drink should be strained into a glass that has been chilled with a mixture of ice cubes and water.

Straws Straws are used as tools in several ways. The straw can be a usable garnish for a drink. The straw gives the drink a finished look and provides the guest a way to sip the drink without touching his or her lips to the side of the glass. The other use for a straw is for sampling the drink. The bartender can dip the straw into the drink and then put a finger over the top of the straw to create a vacuum that will hold the liquid. The bartender can then taste the drink through the open end of the straw. Many bartenders use this technique to make sure that the balance of the drink is correct and that the drink tastes the way it should taste.

Swizzle sticks Swizzle sticks are used for built drinks, especially drinks from the Caribbean. The swizzle stick is used to mix and stir the drink.

INGREDIENTS

Vodka Vodka is a non-aged, clear, distilled spirit with no aroma and no flavor. Vodka can be made from most anything with sugar. Bartenders like vodka because this neutral spirit sells well and mixes into drinks like a dream.

Gin Gin is a non-aged, clear, distilled spirit with a very distinct flavor and aroma. Gin starts off as a neutral spirit. Each gin is different, but most will have juniper berry in the flavor and aroma. Many mixed drinks are made with gin.

Rum Rum is a distilled spirit that can be non-aged or aged. Made from sugar cane, rum is an excellent mixer.

Tequila Tequila is a distilled spirit that can be non-aged or aged. This spirit is made from the agave plant. Unlike all the other spirits that are made from the annual crops of the world, tequila is made from agave, which takes almost a decade to grow. Great planning goes into tequila's production.

Brandy Brandy is a distilled spirit that can be non-aged or aged. Brandy is made from fruit wine, in most cases grape wine. Many popular brandies are aged in casks that give a golden color to the brandy.

Whiskey Whiskey is a distilled spirit that can be non-aged or aged. Whiskey is made from grain beer. All types of grains are used to make whiskey—although certain whiskeys require specific grains.

Liqueurs A liqueur is a sweetened, flavored spirit that is often used as a mixer, although liqueurs can be consumed by themselves before or after a meal. Flavors vary: fruits, nuts, or herbs infuse most of the liqueurs on the market.

Fortified wine Fortified wine is wine with brandy added to raise the alcohol content. Originally this was done to preserve wines during storage and shipping, but the increased alcohol also makes fortified wine a terrific addition to a cocktail.

Fresh juice Cocktails are better with fresh-squeezed juice. Most cocktails that feature juice contain a citrus juice: lime, lemon, orange, or grapefruit. Make sure to have enough to make cocktails for your party. Make sure that cocktails with juice are shaken.

Garnishes Most cocktails have prescriptive garnishes. For example, the Tom Collins always comes with an orange slice and a cocktail cherry, which is also the garnish for the old-fashioned. The Manhattan is garnished with a cocktail cherry, and the horse's neck comes with a long lemon twist. Make sure you know the proper garnishes and have plenty of garnishes for your party.

Some of the recipes you will make will call for simple syrup, which is simple and cheap to make. Some recipes call for sugar and water, but simple syrup will save time and will ensure that the sugar is completely dissolved. Here is a recipe for a good simple syrup to make at home.

$\mathscr{H}$OMEMADE SIMPLE SYRUP

1 cup water
1½ cups sugar

Place both the water and the sugar into a small pot. Bring the mixture to a boil for three minutes; then take the resulting syrup off the heat and let cool. Put the syrup into a plastic bottle and use as needed. Yield: about 2 cups.

Anytime a drink calls for lime juice or lemon juice and simple syrup, you can substitute sour mix. For example, if the drink calls for 1 ounce of lemon juice and ½ ounce simple syrup, then 1½ ounces of sour mix can be used instead. The following is a good sour mix to use at a home bar and builds on the knowledge of making simple syrup.

Homemade Sweet and Sour Mix

1½ cups sugar
1 cup water
1 cup fresh-squeezed lemon juice
½ cup fresh-squeezed lime juice
½ cup fresh-squeezed orange juice

Squeeze enough lemons, limes, and oranges to have the needed quantity of juice. Mix the juice and refrigerate. Make the simple syrup with the sugar and the water by boiling for three minutes. Cool the simple syrup, then add to the fresh-squeezed juice.

Grenadine is a sweet and tart syrup used to flavor and color drinks a shade of red or pink. The origin of the word *grenadine* comes from the French word *grenade*, which means *pomegranate*. This is an easy recipe to make and will elevate drinks beyond the store-bought version.

Homemade Grenadine

1 cup pomegranate juice (no sugar added)
1½ cups sugar
½ teaspoon fresh lemon juice

Pour the sugar and the pomegranate juice into a pot. Warm, stirring the whole time, until the sugar dissolves into the juice. Pull from heat and allow to cool. Once cool, add the lemon juice. Store in bottles or jars under refrigeration. Use as needed. Yield: 2 cups.

There are some very good cocktail cherries on the market. If cherries are in season, you might try making them yourself. Here is an easy recipe that will get you started.

*H*OMEMADE COCKTAIL CHERRIES

40 fresh cherries (sweet or sour, to taste)
¼ teaspoon cinnamon
2 cups plus ¼ cup bourbon (or your favorite spirit)

Pit the cherries. Heat a pan on the stove, pour the cherries into the pan, and sauté in the ¼ cup bourbon. If the cherries catch the flame, remove from the stove until the flame burns out. Add the cinnamon and mix. Pour the cherries into a sanitized jar and cover with bourbon. Allow to cool and refrigerate. Serve with your favorite cocktail that calls for a cocktail cherry.

$\mathcal{H}$OMEMADE ORGEAT SYRUP

1 cup almond milk
1 cup simple syrup
1 teaspoon orange flower water
1 ounce bourbon

Mix the almond milk and simple syrup together. Add the bourbon and orange flower water, stir together, and then let sit for twenty-four hours. Use as directed in cocktails.

GLASSWARE

Champagne flute A champagne flute is a tall drink glass designed to hold sparkling wine. With a narrow opening at the top, the glass effectively holds the CO_2 and releases the gas slowly, which allows for tiny streams of bubbles that float to the top of the glass. This glass is also great for many cocktails, including the Seelbach cocktail and the French 75.

Cocktail glass Also known as a martini glass, this is the perfect vessel for a chilled drink served straight up. The V-shaped glass is iconic.

Highball glass Perfect for long drinks, this tall glass holds ice as well as at least ten ounces of liquid.

Hurricane glass This is an hourglass-shaped glass used for the hurricane cocktail and other drinks.

Margarita glass A glass designed specifically for the margarita, it has a large flat bowl at the top.

Mug This is a large vessel used for beer and cocktails.

Mule mug This distinctive copper mug is traditionally used for the mule family of drinks.

Old-fashioned A glass with straight sides and a flat bottom, it is also known as a low-ball glass or a rocks glass.

Pilsner glass The pilsner glass is perfect for a glass of beer or a beer cocktail.

Pint glass The pint glass is used for beer and other cocktails.

Red wine glass This is a wine glass with a large bowl on top and a long stem.

Shot glass This small glass holds between 1 and 2 ounces or a shot of spirits.

White wine glass This is a wine glass with a small bowl on top and a long stem.

TECHNIQUES

Bartenders use several techniques to make drinks properly. Each drink calls for specific bartending skills. Knowing how to complete drinks using these techniques will increase street credibility for the home bartender.

Blending This technique is the foundation of drinks such as the margarita, daiquiri, or piña colada. Blending is important for incorporating thick dairy products and whole or frozen fruit into a cocktail. Try to use less ice; too much ice will water down the finished drink. A happy medium is to use some ice and some frozen fruit to maximize the flavor of the drink. Crushed ice should always be used for this technique to help extend the life and blades of the blender. When using crushed ice, be sure to blend for twenty seconds, stop, then blend for ten seconds.

Building Building a drink is simply pouring one ingredient into the glass after another until all the ingredients are in the glass. This technique is used for gin and tonics, Moscow mules, Collinses, and screwdrivers.

Layering The layering technique involves the bartender's knowledge of the specific gravity of a liquid. The heavier liquids are used as a base, while the lighter liquids are floated (or layered) on top of the heavier liquids to create a layered appearance in the glass. Examples of layered drinks include the B-52, the tequila sunrise, the black and tan, and the classic pousse-café.

Muddling In this technique the bartender releases flavors by using a muddler to crush sugar, citrus fruit, or herbs before adding ice and alcohol to the drink. Generally, the herb or fruit should be lightly muddled so as not to release the bitter flavors of overmuddled items. The old-fashioned, caipirinha, mint julep, and mojito are examples of muddled drinks.

Shaking The shaking method is used for drinks that need to combine ingredients that might not combine easily in a uniform manner any other way. Shaking will also aerate the cocktail, allowing for a foam or froth on top. Cocktails with citrus juice or egg whites are typically shaken cocktails. Examples of cocktails that use the shaking method are the cosmopolitan, the kamikaze, and the sidecar.

Stirring Stirring is perfect for drinks that are completely made from alcoholic beverages. The purpose of stirring the drink is to make sure that you have a result that is crystal clear. To complete this technique, fill a mixing glass with ice and then pour the ingredients into the glass. Using a barspoon, stir the drink at least forty turns, or until completely chilled. Top the mixing glass with a strainer, and pour the drink into a chilled glass or a glass with ice. The Manhattan, negroni, and martini are examples of stirred cocktails.

COCKTAIL CREATION: A BALANCING ACT

Keep in mind that cocktail creation is a balancing act. A great cocktail is not too sweet, not too sour, and not too bitter. The perfect cocktail is just right. When you see a bartender stick a straw into a drink to syphon out a sip of the cocktail, the bartender is checking for balance in flavor.

A great cocktail to play with is the old-fashioned. The home bartender can play around with the recipe to see how each of the elements plays a part in the overall cocktail creation. In the case of the old-fashioned, the sugar melts into the water and provides the sweet element to the cocktail. Bitters are added to help elevate the flavor of the cocktail and to counter the sugar so the drink is not too sweet. The spirit is added and brings the cocktail together. But wait—what type of spirit? Each spirit will have a different reaction to the overall recipe. The old-fashioned will have a different balance and different flavor based on the spirit.

Another cocktail that the home bartender can play around with is the homemade margarita. This is a splendid example of a "sour" drink. We want the margarita to be sour but not too sour, which is why we balance the drink with sweet—but not too much. This balance in flavor is important.

THREE

Cocktail Recipes

FOR CENTURIES, ROYALS AND NOBLES have used alcohol to celebrate. The celebrations include, but are not limited to, weddings, births, deaths, coronations, and preparing for battle. Ensuring the supply of alcohol is very important, and royal warrants are issued to liquor companies that are the favorites of the royals. These warrants are usually indicated on the bottle.

All alcoholic beverages start with fermentation. During fermentation, yeast converts sugar into alcohol and carbon dioxide. Fermentation creates both beer and wine. Beer is made from a liquid laced primarily with grains like barley, rice, and corn. Wine is made from the liquids from fruit. Fermented beverages like beer and wine can be served in cocktails, but they can also be distilled into a spirit at a higher alcohol by volume. Spirits fall into three categories: (1) clear spirits; (2) spirits that are sometimes clear and sometimes brown; and (3) brown spirits. Each spirit category is represented in this chapter. First are the clear spirits, vodka and gin. Then are the spirits that come both clear and brown, rum and tequila (and mescal), followed by the brown spirits, brandy and whiskey. Finally, there are other cocktails that are made with wine, beer, or liqueurs.

JOE GILMORE, THE KING OF BARMEN AND THE BARMAN TO KINGS

Joseph "Joe" Patrick Gilmore was the King of Barmen and the Barman to Kings. During his long career at the Savoy Hotel's American Bar, the native Irishman served five generations of British royals, other royals, and numerous stars of stage and recording, including Grace Kelly, who fell into more than one category as an Academy Award–winning actress and the princess consort of Monaco. Gilmore was born in Belfast, Northern Ireland, on May 19, 1922. He joined the Savoy's American Bar in 1940 as a trainee barman. Gilmore was named the head barman in 1955, a position he held until he retired in 1976. He was known for his sharp memory and attention to detail. For example, King Umberto of Italy did not have to ask for a second cherry in his Manhattan; Gilmore always remembered. Over his career, Gilmore created cocktails to honor the Prince of Wales (Prince Charles); the Princess Royal (Princess Anne); Queen Elizabeth the Queen Mother; the Duke of York (Prince Andrew); Sarah, Duchess of York; big-screen royal Julie Andrews; and Sir Winston Churchill, whose grandfather was the 7th Duke of Marlborough. Outside of his amazing creations and his memory, Gilmore was known for his discretion. Gilmore was trusted by the British royal family. Princess Margaret, Countess of Snowdon, would often fly Gilmore to her private residence Les Jolies Eaux on the Island of Mustique in Saint Vincent and the Grenadines. After a long and distinguished career, Gilmore passed away December 18, 2015, at the age of ninety-three.

JOE GILMORE'S CREATIONS
FOR ROYALS AND NOBLES

The Prince of Wales (Prince Charles) is the longest-serving Prince of Wales. He is the heir to his mother, Queen Elizabeth II. His full name is Charles Phillip Arthur George. If he succeeds his mother, he will most likely rule as George VII. He married Lady Diana Spencer, and they had Prince William, Duke of Cambridge, and Prince Harry, Duke of Sussex. The marriage ended in divorce. After Princess Diana's death, Prince Charles married his longtime love, Camilla Parker-Bowles, who is now referred to as Camilla, Duchess of Cornwall. Gilmore created this drink in 1958 to honor Prince Charles on his investiture as the Prince of Wales.

$\mathscr{P}$RINCE OF WALES

1 sugar cube
1 strawberry
1 ounce cherry brandy
1 ounce lemon juice
4 ounces sparkling wine

Add ice and water to a champagne flute to chill the glass. Hull the strawberry. Add ice to the tin side of a Boston shaker. In the mixing glass, add the sugar cube, strawberry, lemon juice, and cherry brandy. Muddle the ingredients together. Pour the contents of the mixing glass into the iced tin and secure the glass to the tin. Shake the contents until the ice sounds different and the contents are cold. Open the Boston shaker. Empty the champagne flute, then strain the contents of the shaker into the empty glass. Top the cocktail with sparkling wine. Serve.

The second child of Queen Elizabeth II and Prince Phillip is Princess Anne, the Princess Royal, a title she received in 1987. She is the grand master of the Royal Victorian Order. The Princess Royal and her first husband, Captain Mark Phillips, married in 1973. They have two children, Peter Phillips and Zara Tindall, the only two of the queen's grandchildren not to hold a royal or noble title because titles normally do not pass through the female line (there are a few exceptions). The couple divorced in 1992. The Princess Royal remarried Sir Timothy Laurence. Joe Gilmore created this cocktail to honor the princess and Phillips on their wedding day.

GOLDEN DOUBLET

¾ ounce orange juice
¼ ounce lime juice
1 ounce Grand Marnier
3 ounces sparkling wine

Add ice and water to a champagne coupe to chill the glass. Add ice to the tin side of a Boston shaker. In the mixing glass, add orange juice, lime juice, and Grand Marnier. Pour the contents of the mixing glass into the iced tin and secure the glass to the tin. Shake the contents until the ice sounds different and the contents are cold. Open the Boston shaker. Empty the champagne coupe, then strain the contents of the shaker into the empty glass. Top the cocktail with sparkling wine. Serve.

Queen Elizabeth the Queen Mother was the consort to King George VI and mother of Queen Elizabeth II and Princess Margaret, Countess of Snowdon. The queen mother's father was Claude Bowes-Lyon, the 14th Earl of Strathmore and Kinghorne. The queen mother lived to 101. Joe Gilmore created this cocktail to honor the last empress of India.

AVOY ROYALE

½ peach
2 strawberries
Sugar cube
4 ounces sparkling wine

Add ice and water to a champagne flute to chill the glass. In a blender, add the peach, strawberries, and sugar cube. Blend until smooth. Empty the champagne flute, then strain the contents of the shaker into the empty glass. Top the cocktail with sparkling wine. Serve.

Sir Winston Churchill is best known for his role as the British prime minister during World War II. Churchill was the son of Lord Randolph Churchill and his American bride, Lady Jennie (Jerome) Churchill. Lord Randolph was the fifth child and third son of His Grace John Spencer-Churchill, the 7th Duke of Marlborough, and his consort, Frances, Duchess of Marlborough. Joe Gilmore created this cocktail to honor the famous prime minister.

HURCHILL

1½ ounces Scotch whisky
½ ounce lime juice
½ ounce sweet vermouth
½ ounce Cointreau

Add ice and water to a cocktail glass to chill the glass. Add ice to the tin side of a Boston shaker. In the mixing glass, add Scotch whisky, lime juice, sweet vermouth, and Cointreau. Pour the contents of the mixing glass into the iced tin and secure the glass to the tin. Shake the contents until the ice sounds different and the contents are cold. Open the Boston shaker. Empty the cocktail glass, then strain the contents of the shaker into the empty glass. Serve.

Joe Gilmore created this cocktail to honor Churchill on his eightieth birthday in 1955.

OUR SCORE

1½ ounces brandy
1 ounce Lillet
½ ounce Yellow Chartreuse

Add ice and water to a cocktail glass to chill the glass. Add ice to the tin side of a Boston shaker. In the mixing glass, add brandy, Lillet, and Yellow Chartreuse. Pour the contents of the mixing glass into the iced tin and secure the glass to the tin. Shake the contents until the ice sounds different and the contents are cold. Open the Boston shaker. Empty the cocktail glass, then strain the contents of the shaker into the empty glass. Serve.

Joe Gilmore created this cocktail in honor of Churchill on his ninetieth birthday in 1965.

$\mathcal{T}$HE BLENHEIM
(FOUR SCORE AND TEN)

1½ ounces brandy
1 ounce Yellow Chartreuse
½ ounce Lillet
½ ounce orange juice
½ ounce Dubonnet

Add ice and water to a cocktail glass to chill the glass. Add ice to the tin side of a Boston shaker. In the mixing glass, add brandy, Yellow Chartreuse, Lillet, orange juice, and Dubonnet. Pour the contents of the mixing glass into the iced tin and secure the glass to the tin. Shake the contents until the ice sounds different and the contents are cold. Open the Boston shaker. Empty the cocktail glass, then strain the contents of the shaker into the empty glass. Serve.

Dame Julie Andrews is an award-winning English actress who is known to many as the queen of Genovia from her big-screen performance in *The Princess Diaries* and as the voice of Queen Lillian in the *Shrek* trilogy. This royal persona should not be surprising; she began her film career as the voice of

Princess Zeila in *La Rosa di Bagdad*. Andrews also played Queen Guinevere in *Camelot* on Broadway. She became silver screen royalty when she was awarded an Academy Award for the title role in *Mary Poppins* in 1965 and a Golden Globe for the role of Maria Von Trapp in *The Sound of Music* in 1966. In 2000, Andrews was honored by HM Queen Elizabeth II as a Dame in the Most Excellent Order of the British Empire. Gilmore honored her with a cocktail for her Broadway performance in *My Fair Lady* in 1956.

MY FAIR LADY

¾ ounce gin
¾ ounce lemon juice
¾ ounce orange juice
¾ ounce strawberry simple syrup
½ ounce egg white

Add ice and water to a cocktail to chill the glass. Add ice to the tin side of a Boston shaker. In the mixing glass, add the gin, lemon juice, orange juice, strawberry simple syrup, and egg white. Pour the contents of the mixing glass into the iced tin and secure the glass to the tin. Shake the contents until the ice sounds different and the contents are cold. Open the Boston shaker. Empty the cocktail glass, then strain the contents of the shaker into the empty glass. Serve.

MORE ROYAL CREATIONS

VODKA COCKTAILS

Vodka is the choice of bartenders. Vodka is the perfect spirit for a royal and for a bartender, albeit for different reasons.

Vodka is colorless and flavorless and has little aroma. In other words, the spirit is neutral once vodka is mixed into a cocktail, which allows maximum creativity from the bartender and maximum discretion for the royal. This lack of distinguishable character is achieved by distilling vodka to a higher alcohol by volume and then watering it down to the desired proof. Smirnoff capitalized on this in 1953, creating an ad campaign that stated, "It leaves you breathless!" The campaign was a play on words. The vodka is undetectable when mixed with other beverages such as orange juice, tomato juice, or tonic water. Most other spirits can be detected on the breath of the person consuming that spirit. Vodka can be made from anything, but most vodkas are made from grains or potatoes. Today, vodka is one of the most popular spirits with bar customers, and bartenders love it too because, as many bartenders will tell you, "Vodka pays the bills."

King Henry II of England aspired to be an emperor. He almost succeeded, and the area that he ruled is referred to as the Angevin Empire. He inherited the throne of England through his mother, who was the daughter of Henry I. He inherited the counties of Anjou, Touraine, and Maine and the Duchy of Normandy from his father, Geoffrey Plantagenet. Then Henry married Eleanor of Aquitaine, former consort to King Louis VII of France, which brought the Duchy of Aquitaine under his control. He added Wales, Ireland, and Scotland by conquest. Henry and Eleanor had many children, three of whom would later rule England: Henry (the Young King), Richard, and John. However, Henry was known for his many conflicts with family and friends. One of those friends was Thomas Becket, who Henry appointed Lord Chancellor and then later Archbishop of Canterbury. Once Thomas was archbishop, the two friends did not always see eye to eye and engaged in open conflict. Years later, Henry is reported to have said to four knights, "What miserable drones and traitors have I nourished and promoted in my household, who let their lord be treated with such shameful contempt by a low-born clerk," and "Will no one rid me of this turbulent priest?" The four knights left for the Cathedral at Canterbury and killed Becket in the cathedral as he celebrated mass. Henry would perform public penance for Becket's death—yes, even kings perform penance. As a martyr, the former archbishop would become Saint Thomas of Canterbury.

BSOLUTION

1 ounce vodka
5 ounces sparkling wine
Lemon twist

Add ice and water to a champagne flute to chill the glass. After a minute, empty the champagne flute, then pour the vodka into the glass. Top the cocktail with sparkling wine. Garnish with a lemon twist. Serve.

Alexander III of Macedon is known for his generalship, conquering most of Greece, modern-day Turkey, Egypt, the Middle East, and part of India. Called Alexander the Great, he was the son of King Phillip II of Macedon and was tutored by Aristotle. After Phillip's assassination, Alexander was declared king at age twenty. He had his army set out on a conquest of other kingdoms and countries. His empire came to an end at the age of thirty-two, when he passed away after a short illness. Some have suggested that he was poisoned.

ALEXANDER THE GREAT

1½ ounces vodka
½ ounce white crème de cacao
½ ounce coffee liqueur
½ ounce cream

Add ice and water to a highball glass to chill the glass. Add ice to the tin side of a Boston shaker. In the mixing glass, add vodka, white crème de cacao, coffee liqueur, and cream. Pour the contents of the mixing glass into the iced tin and secure the glass to the tin. Shake the contents until the ice sounds different and the contents are cold. Open the Boston shaker. Empty the highball glass and then refill the glass with ice. Then strain the contents of the shaker into the glass. Serve.

At the beginning of World War II, many in the British government felt that for the safety of Princess Elizabeth and her sister Princess Margaret, they should leave Britain for Canada. The future queen mother said, "The children will not leave unless I do. I shall not leave unless their father does, and the king will not leave the country in any circumstances whatever." The royal family stayed in Britain throughout the war. During World War II, the future Queen Elizabeth II trained to be an ambulance driver and mechanic with the Auxiliary Territorial Service.

MBULANCE

2 ounces vodka
1 ounce coffee liqueur
1½ ounces coffee
3 ounces cola

Add ice to a Collins glass to chill the glass. Add the vodka, coffee liqueur, coffee, and cola. Stir and serve.

Avalon means "the Island of Apples" and is the island where King Arthur died. However, some legends hold that King Arthur never died but only traveled to Avalon to recover from his wounds and will be back to lead his people again—thus, the title of T. H. White's book *The Once and Future King*. Some also claim that this island is where the sword Excalibur was forged. Traditionally, the hill Glastonbury Tor in Southwest England has been identified as the former island.

$\mathscr{A}$VALON

1½ ounces vodka
½ ounce crème de banana
3 ounces apple juice
¾ ounce lemon juice
¾ ounce lemonade
Cucumber skin spiral
Cocktail cherry

Add ice to a Collins glass. Add the vodka, lemon juice, apple juice, and crème de banana, and finish with the lemonade. Stir slightly. Garnish with the cucumber and cherry. Serve.

The story of Beowulf is one of the oldest surviving pieces of English literature. The story follows the Geats hero Beowulf as he supports King Hrothgar of the Danes against an attack on the king's mead hall. The poem continues, following Beowulf's ascension to king of the Geats.

EOWULF

1 ounce blue curaçao
1 ounce vodka

Put a shot glass on the bar or drip mat. Add ice to the tin side of a Boston shaker. In the mixing glass, add blue curaçao and vodka. Pour the contents of the mixing glass into the iced tin and secure the glass to the tin. Shake the contents until the ice sounds different and the contents are cold. Open the Boston shaker. Strain the contents of the shaker into the shot glass. Serve.

Morgan le Fay is the half sister in addition to the sometime seductress of King Arthur. Her role in the Arthurian legend has changed over the years. Morgan is sometimes the villain and sometimes the savior of Arthur when he is wounded in battle by their son, Sir Mordred.

BLACK MAGIC

½ ounce vodka
½ ounce elderflower liqueur
2 ounces sparkling wine
4 ounces Kombucha black currant

Add ice to an old-fashioned glass. Add the vodka, elder-flower, sparkling wine, and Kombucha black currant to the old-fashioned glass. Stir. Serve.

Queen Mary of England and Ireland was the eldest daughter of Henry VIII and his first wife, Catherine of Aragon. After her half brother Edward VI died at the young age of fifteen and a short-lived palace coup that installed Lady Jane Grey as queen was put down, Mary was crowned queen of England and Ireland. Mary also served as the queen consort to Phillip II of Spain. Mary was a Roman Catholic, but her father broke from the Catholic Church to form the Church of England. Mary was determined to return the county back to the Catholic Church by force if necessary. That is how she claimed the nickname Bloody Mary. She would only rule for less than five years before passing away with no children from what most likely was cancer. She was succeeded by her half sister Elizabeth I, who solidified the Church of England as the church in England. Phillip immediately proposed marriage to Elizabeth, who turned him down.

LOODY MARY

1½ ounces vodka
3 ounces tomato juice
½ ounce lemon juice
3 dashes Worcestershire sauce
2 dashes Tabasco sauce
1 dash celery salt
1 dash pepper
Celery stalk with cheese and sausage tacked to the celery
Lime wedge

Add ice to a highball glass. Add the vodka, tomato juice, lemon juice, Worcestershire sauce, Tabasco sauce, celery salt, and pepper. Stir. Add celery stalk and lime wedge as a garnish. Serve.

Similar to the Bloody Mary is the Caesar, a drink common in Canada. The cocktail is basically a Bloody Mary with clam juice. Julius Caesar lends his name to this drink and the words *tzar*, *czar*, *kaiser*, and, of course, *caesar*, which is synonymous with *emperor*.

AESAR

1½ ounces vodka
4 ounces Clamato juice
4 dashes Worcestershire sauce
2 dashes Tabasco sauce
1 dash celery salt
1 dash pepper
Celery stalk
Lime wedge

Add ice to a highball glass. Add the vodka, Clamato juice, Worcestershire sauce, Tabasco sauce, celery salt, and pepper. Stir. Add celery stalk and lime wedge as a garnish. Serve.

Queen Isabella I of Castile and King Ferdinand II of Aragon were the power couple of the fourteenth century—perhaps the original power couple. The marriage between these two monarchs effectively united all of Spain. In addition, Isabella and Ferdinand sponsored Christopher Columbus in what would become his exploration of the New World, most of which they would claim for Spain.

CATHOLIC CORONATION

1 ounce vodka
½ ounce amaretto
½ ounce butterscotch schnapps
½ ounce Frangelico
½ ounce milk

Add ice and water to a cocktail glass to chill the glass. Add ice to the tin side of a Boston shaker. In the mixing glass, add vodka, amaretto, butterscotch schnapps, Frangelico, and milk. Pour the contents of the mixing glass into the iced tin and secure the glass to the tin. Shake the contents until the ice sounds different and the contents are cold. Open the Boston shaker. Empty the cocktail glass, then strain the contents of the shaker into the empty glass. Serve.

Denmark is the scene for an epic squabble over a throne in William Shakespeare's play *Hamlet*. The stage is set and pits Prince Hamlet, the son of a murdered king, against the king's killer, who is none other than the current king, Claudius, the murdered king's brother and Hamlet's uncle. In an added complication, Claudius married Hamlet's mother, the queen consort to the dead king. The tragedy outlines the destruction of the Danish royal family.

AMLET

1 ounce vodka
½ ounce Campari
4 ounces orange juice

Add ice to a Collins glass. Add ice to the tin side of a Boston shaker. In the mixing glass, add vodka, Campari, and orange juice. Pour the contents of the mixing glass into the iced tin and secure the glass to the tin. Shake the contents until the ice sounds different and the contents are cold. Open the Boston shaker. Strain the contents of the shaker into the ice-filled glass. Serve.

The Holy Grail is the cup, chalice, or container used as the container for the wine at the Last Supper and later used by Joseph of Arimathea to catch the blood of Christ at the crucifixion. According to legend, Joseph of Arimathea later took the grail to England on the Island of Britain. Many knights, both real and legendary, sought the grail for the glory of God . . . or because many believe the grail has the power to extend life and turn want into abundance. Several people believe that they have discovered the grail. Is this the secret behind the long life of many in the royal family?

OLY GRAIL

1 ounce vodka
1 ounce Campari
½ ounce apricot brandy
1½ ounces orange juice
½ ounce egg white

Add ice and water to a cocktail glass to chill the glass. Add ice to the tin side of a Boston shaker. In the mixing glass, add vodka, Campari, apricot brandy, orange juice, and egg white. Pour the contents of the mixing glass into the iced tin and secure the glass to the tin. Shake the contents until the ice sounds different and the contents are cold. Open the Boston shaker. Empty the cocktail glass, then strain the contents of the shaker into the empty glass. Serve.

Reza Pahlavi is the man who could be Shahanshah of Iran. *Shahanshah* translates into English as "King of Kings" or "Emperor." Pahlavi is the last crown prince of Iran, as his father was Mohammad Reza Pahlavi, the last Shahanshah of Iran.

He lost his empire during the Iranian Revolution in 1979 but became the head of the House of Pahlavi in 1980 upon his father's death. Today, Pahlavi lives in the United States with his wife and three daughters.

ERSIAN PRINCE

1 ounce vodka
1 ounce rum
1 ounce sweet and sour mix
1 ounce orange juice
1 ounce lemon-lime soda

Add ice to a highball glass. Add the vodka, rum, sweet and sour mix, orange juice, and lemon-lime soda. Serve.

King Haakon VII of Norway was never a prince of Norway. He was a Danish prince, the second son of the future King Frederick VIII of Denmark and his consort, Louise. Born Prince Carl of Denmark, Haakon VII was elected to be king of Norway as the joint United Kingdoms of Sweden and Norway dissolved in 1905, becoming two distinct kingdoms. Haakon was the perfect king for Norway. His mother was the only daughter of King Charles XV of Sweden. Haakon married Princess Maud of Wales, the daughter of British King Edward VII and his consort, Alexandria of Denmark. The connections to the Swedish, British, and Danish crowns proved important connections during the two World Wars. In a rare twist of fate, Haakon became king of Norway before his father became king of Denmark. Haakon ruled for almost fifty-two years, during which time Denmark had four kings, including his father, brother, and nephew. When Germany invaded Norway during World War II, the king threatened to abdicate if the Norwegian government collaborated with the Nazis. The story is featured in the 2016 film *The King's Choice*.

PRINCE OF NORWAY

¾ ounce vodka
¾ ounce apricot brandy
¼ ounce lime juice
5 ounces lemon-lime soda

Add ice to a highball glass. Add vodka, apricot brandy, lime juice, and lemon-lime soda. Serve.

During World War I, there was no aviator more feared than Manfred von Richthofen, who was better known as the Red Baron. During his short flying career, he was credited with eighty combat victories. The Red Baron was shot down April 21, 1918, after a dogfight. He was able to land his plane before he passed away.

RED BARON

2 ounces vodka
5 ounces orange juice
½ ounce grenadine

Add ice to a highball glass. Add vodka, orange juice, and grenadine. Serve.

Robin Hood, or Robin of Loxley (or Locksley), is both a historical and fictional character and is forever linked with the noble title of the Earl of Huntingdon. The title dates back to 1065, but the most recent creation (the seventh) was an honor bestowed on George Hastings in 1529 by King Henry VIII. The family seems to have embraced the Huntingdon connection with the hero. The current Earl is William Edward Robin Hood Hastings-Bass, 17th Earl of Huntingdon. His heir is his brother, the Hon. John Peter Robin Hood Hastings-Bass.

ROBIN HOOD

½ ounce vodka
½ ounce gold tequila
1 dashes crème de banana
1½ ounces orange juice
1 ounce pineapple juice

Add ice and water to a cocktail glass to chill the glass. Add ice to the tin side of a Boston shaker. In the mixing glass, add vodka, tequila, crème de banana, orange juice, and pineapple juice. Pour the contents of the mixing glass into the iced tin and secure the glass to the tin. Shake the contents until the ice sounds different and the contents are cold. Open the Boston shaker. Empty the cocktail glass, then strain the contents of the shaker into the empty glass. Serve.

Love is blind. The best marriages include passion. Although many royal weddings happen as part of a larger diplomatic plan, sometimes royals or nobles enter into a morganatic marriage, or a marriage between people who do not share the same social status. Sometimes this prevents titles and privileges being passed to the spouse or children produced from the marriage. While these were looked down on in the past (a view of morganatic marriages that led to many marriages between cousins), in recent years, royals mixing with commoners has become more acceptable.

OYAL PASSION

1½ ounces vodka
1 ounce raspberry liqueur
1 ounce passion fruit juice

Add ice and water to a cocktail glass to chill the glass. Add ice to the tin side of a Boston shaker. In the mixing glass, add vodka, raspberry liqueur, and passion fruit juice. Pour the contents of the mixing glass into the iced tin and secure the glass to the tin. Shake the contents until the ice sounds different and the contents are cold. Open the Boston shaker. Empty the cocktail glass, then strain the contents of the shaker into the empty glass. Serve.

During her sixty-three-year reign, Queen Victoria survived eight assassination attempts. The first came during an open-air carriage trip with Victoria's prince consort, Albert. The prince later wrote that the shots were taken only six paces away from the couple. The first shot surprised the couple but missed. Before the second shot, Albert reacted, pulling the pregnant Victoria to safety. There was speculation that the queen's uncle, the Duke of Cumberland, who was also the

King of Hanover, was behind the assassination attempt. If the bullets had hit their mark, Cumberland would have inherited the crown.

$\mathcal{V}$ICTORIA'S SHOT

⅔ ounce vodka
⅔ ounce passion fruit liqueur
⅓ ounce pineapple juice
Dash simple syrup
Dash lime juice

Prepare a shot glass. Add ice to the tin side of a Boston shaker. In the mixing glass, add vodka, passion fruit liqueur, pineapple juice, simple syrup, and lime juice. Pour the contents of the mixing glass into the iced tin and secure the glass to the tin. Shake the contents until the ice sounds different and the contents are cold. Open the Boston shaker. Strain the contents of the shaker into the empty shot glass. Serve.

Vlad the Impaler (Vlad III) was the son of Vlad Dracul (Vlad II). Both were rulers of the principality of Wallachia in the 1400s. Vlad the Impaler took his name from the practice of impaling his enemies. Impalement involved driving a large spear through the body and leaving the victim there to die. This method of torturous death was seen as a good deterrent to crossing the current ruler.

$\mathscr{V}$LAD THE IMPALER

2 ounces vodka
¾ ounce peach schnapps
4 ounces cranberry cocktail juice

Add ice to a Collins glass. Add ice to the tin side of a Boston shaker. In the mixing glass, add vodka, peach schnapps, and cranberry cocktail juice. Pour the contents of the mixing glass into the iced tin and secure the glass to the tin. Shake the contents until the ice sounds different and the contents are cold. Open the Boston shaker. Strain the contents of the shaker into the empty glass. Serve.

Disney has told the story of *Beauty and the Beast*, the tale of a prince with a physical ailment that turns him into a beast. This fairy tale may be based on a real-life Spaniard, Petrus Gonsalvus, who suffered from hypertrichosis or excessive hair growth—in Petrus's case, all over his body. He traveled among the European royal court in the early 1500s. He married and had seven children, four of whom inherited their father's affliction. This cocktail was on the Arnaud's cocktail menu.

$\mathscr{B}$EAUTY AND THE BEAST

1½ ounces vodka
1½ ounces crème de cassis
2 dashes of lemon juice
5 dashes grenadine

Add ice and water to a cocktail glass to chill the glass. Add ice to the tin side of a Boston shaker. In the mixing glass, add vodka, crème de cassis, lemon juice, and grenadine. Pour the contents of the mixing glass into the iced tin and secure the glass to the tin. Shake the contents until the ice sounds different and the contents are cold. Open the Boston shaker. Empty the cocktail glass, then strain the contents of the shaker into the empty glass. Serve.

Barbara Bach is best known as a model and actress. She is now also called Lady Starkey, a courtesy title as the wife of Sir Richard Starkey, who is better known as Ringo Starr from the Beatles. Starr was knighted in 2018. Before her marriage to Starr, Bach was married to Count Augusto Gregorini from 1966 to 1978, during which time she was by courtesy a countess.

BARBARA

1 ounce vodka
1 ounce coffee liqueur
1 ounce cream
Nutmeg

Fill a cocktail glass with ice and water to chill. Fill the tin side of a Boston shaker with ice. Add the vodka, coffee liqueur, and cream into the glass side of the shaker, then pour the liquid into the tin and attach the two sides. Shake until the combination is cold. Discard the ice and water in the cocktail glass. Strain the cocktail into the cocktail glass and garnish with nutmeg. Serve.

With few exceptions, to inherit title, land, and power, a royal must be legitimate. An illegitimate child (one born outside of marriage) is considered a royal bastard. A great example of an exception is William the Conqueror, who was the first Norman King of England. Before he was known as "the Conqueror," William was known as William the Bastard. Many kings and princes have fathered a bastard or many bastards. King Charles II fathered twenty, King James II fathered thirteen, King William IV fathered eleven, King Alfonso XIII of Spain fathered at least six, and more recently Prince Albert II, the Prince of Monaco, fathered at least two. However, in Britain, Queen Victoria put an end to recognizing royal bastards—even though many exist.

ASTARDLY

1½ ounces vodka
1½ ounces blackberry liqueur
¼ ounce vanilla liqueur
¼ ounce amaretto

Add ice and water to a cocktail glass to chill the glass. Add ice to the tin side of a Boston shaker. In the mixing glass, add vodka, blackberry liqueur, vanilla liqueur, and amaretto. Pour the contents of the mixing glass into the iced tin and secure the glass to the tin. Shake the contents until the ice sounds different and the contents are cold. Open the Boston shaker. Empty the cocktail then strain the contents of the shaker into the empty glass. Serve.

GIN COCKTAILS

Gin starts as a neutral spirit, similar to vodka, but the spirit is exposed to a proprietary brand-specific mixture of seeds, roots, barks, herbs, and spices, with the most common being juniper berries. Gin remains a clear spirit. Many excellent cocktails rely on gin's specific flavor.

Queen Elizabeth is known to have a prelunch cocktail of gin and Dubonnet. The queen mother was also known to have a similar cocktail before lunch. Could this cocktail be the secret to the long lives of both queens?

$\mathcal{Q}$UEEN ELIZABETH II AND QUEEN ELIZABETH THE QUEEN MOTHER COCKTAIL

1 ounce gin
2 ounces Dubonnet
Lemon slice
2 ice cubes

Add ice and water to a cocktail glass to chill the glass. Add ice to the mixing glass, then add gin and Dubonnet. Stir at least forty times. Empty the cocktail glass. Add the lemon slice and two ice cubes to the glass. Strain the contents of the shaker into the empty glass. Serve.

Queen Elizabeth II enjoyed a coronation at the tender age of twenty-six, after succeeding her father, George VI, at age twenty-five. Part of the coronation ceremony calls for anointing the monarch with holy oil. The reserve oil that was used for her father was lost during the Germany bombing of World War II, and the company that produced the holy oil was out of business. The palace found a chemist to make a fresh batch of holy oil based on a recipe from the time of Charles I. After the coronation, the British poet Robert Graves enjoyed an audience with the newly crowned queen and said, "The holy oil has taken for that girl. It worked for her all right."

$\mathscr{C}$ORONATION COCKTAIL #2

1 ounce gin
1 ounce dry vermouth
1 ounce Dubonnet
Lemon twist

Add ice and water to a cocktail glass to chill the glass. Add ice to the mixing glass then add gin, dry vermouth, and Dubonnet. Stir at least forty times. Strain the contents of the shaker into the empty glass. Garnish with a lemon twist. Serve.

Westminster Abbey has been the site of all English and later British coronations since William the Conqueror. Even though the church is commonly known as an abbey, technically it is no longer an abbey, and it is not classified as a cathedral because it is not the seat of a bishop. Westminster Abbey holds a specific status as a Royal Peculiar, or a church that is outside of the jurisdiction of a diocese and is under the direct control of the monarch. Other churches that hold this same status include the Church of St. Edward King and Martyr in Cambridge, Chapel Royal in Edinburgh, and St. George's Chapel at Windsor Castle.

$\mathscr{A}$BBEY IN THE CITY

2 ounces London dry gin
1 ounce port wine
1 ounce orange juice
3 dashes orange bitters

Add ice and water to a cocktail glass to chill the glass. Add ice to the tin side of a Boston shaker. In the mixing glass, add gin, port, orange juice, and bitters. Pour the contents of the mixing glass into the iced tin and secure the glass to the tin. Shake the contents until the ice sounds different and the contents are cold. Open the Boston shaker. Empty the cocktail glass, then strain the contents of the shaker into the empty glass. Serve.

As the daughter of Tony Curtis and Janet Leigh, Jamie Lee Curtis was already a Hollywood princess when she was introduced to movie-going audiences in the film *Halloween*. Following in the footsteps of her mother, she was quickly dubbed the "scream queen." In 1984, she married Christopher Guest of *Spinal Tap* fame. Fast-forward to 1996, when Guest succeeded his father as the 5th Baron Haden-Guest, making his wife, by courtesy, the Right Honourable Lady Haden-Guest.

BARON COCKTAIL

1½ ounces gin
½ ounce dry vermouth
¼ ounce triple sec
Splash sweet vermouth
1 lemon wheel

Add ice and water to a cocktail glass to chill the glass. Add ice to the tin side of a Boston shaker. In the mixing glass, add gin, dry vermouth, sweet vermouth, and triple sec. Pour the contents of the mixing glass into the iced tin and secure the glass to the tin. Shake the contents until the ice sounds different and the contents are cold. Open the Boston shaker. Empty the cocktail glass, then strain the contents of the shaker into the empty glass. Garnish with a lemon wheel. Serve.

The word *bijou* means *jewel*. In 2018, the Swedish crown jewels were stolen from their display in a cathedral near Stockholm. The thieves took two crowns and an orb, valued in the millions of dollars altogether, and escaped across the water in a speedboat. The notoriety of the jewels made them impossible to sell. In January 2019, the jewels turned up on top of a garbage can in Stockholm. The same cannot be said of the Irish crown jewels, which were stolen in 1907 from their home in Dublin. Irish authorities as well as Scotland Yard were called out to solve the case, but no one was ever charged with the crime and the jewels were never recovered.

IJOU

1 ounce gin
1 ounce sweet vermouth
1 ounce Green Chartreuse
1 dash orange bitters
Lemon twist
Cocktail cherry

Add ice and water to a cocktail glass to chill the glass. Add ice to the tin side of a Boston shaker. In the mixing glass, add ice, and then add gin, sweet vermouth, Green Chartreuse, and orange bitters. Stir at least forty times, then strain into the cocktail glass. Garnish with a lemon twist and a cocktail cherry. Serve.

One of the symbols of the highest orders of knighthood is a riband, or sash that runs across the chest of the knight from shoulder to hip. A blue riband might suggest any one of the following knightly orders: Order of the Garter (Great Britain), Order of the Tower and Sword (Portuguese), Order of the Holy Spirit (France—also known as Le Cordon Bleu), Royal Order of the Seraphim (Sweden), Order of St. Patrick (British—Ireland), Order of St. Andrew (Russia), Order of the White Eagle (Poland), and Order of the Southern Cross (Brazil).

BLUE RIBAND

1 ounce gin
1 ounce Cointreau
¾ ounce blue curaçao
Orange twist

Add ice and water to a cocktail glass to chill the glass. Add ice to the tin side of a Boston shaker. In the mixing glass, add gin, Cointreau, and blue curaçao. Pour the contents of the mixing glass into the iced tin and secure the glass to the tin. Shake the contents until the ice sounds different and the contents are cold. Open the Boston shaker. Empty the cocktail glass, then strain the contents of the shaker into the empty glass. Garnish with an orange twist. Serve.

The following is a good cocktail for any coronation. Edward VII was a man happy to become king. His mother, Victoria, had ruled Great Britain and the British empire for more than sixty-three years. As Prince of Wales, Edward said at his mother's Diamond Jubilee, "It's all very well about the Eternal Father. But what about my eternal mother?" He acceded to the throne in 1901, but Edward's coronation was delayed because of an emergency appendectomy. In 1902, when his grandchildren visited him in his regalia for the coronation, he said to them, "Am I not a funny-looking old man?"

ORONATION COCKTAIL

1 ounce gin
1 ounce dry vermouth
1 ounce Dubonnet Blonde
Lemon twist

Add ice and water to a cocktail glass to chill the glass. Add ice to the tin side of a Boston shaker. In the mixing glass, add gin, dry vermouth, and Dubonnet Blonde. Pour the contents of the mixing glass into the iced tin and secure the glass to the tin. Shake the contents until the ice sounds different and the contents are cold. Open the Boston shaker. Empty the cocktail glass, then strain the contents of the shaker into the empty glass. Garnish with a lemon twist. Serve.

During the Middle Ages, the crossbow was an important weapon. It was used in the Battle of Hastings in 1066 and was used until replaced by firearms in the 1500s.

CROSSBOW

1½ ounces gin
1 ounce white crème de cacao
1 ounce triple sec

Add ice and water to a cocktail glass to chill the glass. Add ice to the tin side of a Boston shaker. In the mixing glass, add gin, white crème de cacao, and triple sec. Pour the contents of the mixing glass into the iced tin and secure the glass to the tin. Shake the contents until the ice sounds different and the contents are cold. Open the Boston shaker. Empty the cocktail glass, then strain the contents of the shaker into the empty glass. Serve.

Japan is the last empire remaining in the world today. Many of the world's empires came to an end at the end of World War I and others at the end of World War II. The British empire ended in the 1950s, but the Japanese emperors continued in a 2,500-year tradition. In 2019, His Imperial Majesty Naruhito acceded to the Chrysanthemum throne, becoming the 126th emperor of Japan.

MPIRE

1½ ounces gin
¾ ounce apricot brandy
½ ounce Calvados

Add ice and water to a cocktail glass to chill the glass. Add ice to the tin side of a Boston shaker. In the mixing glass, add gin, apricot brandy, and Calvados. Pour the contents of the mixing glass into the iced tin and secure the glass to the tin. Shake the contents until the ice sounds different and the contents are cold. Open the Boston shaker. Empty the cocktail glass, then strain the contents of the shaker into the empty glass. Serve.

The Battle of Agincourt took place on October 25 (St. Crispin's Day), 1415. Henry V of England claimed that he was the rightful heir to the French throne. This was during a period of time in England and France called the Hundred Years' War (which actually lasted about 116 years). Even though the French outnumbered the English by a significant number of soldiers, at the end of the day the triumph was overwhelmingly English. The French advanced into mud, adding weight to their heavy armor. They were sitting ducks, and the English took full advantage of the situation. Henry was joined by his brother, Humphrey, Duke of Gloucester, and cousin Edward, Duke of York, who was killed in the battle. The battle is depicted in William Shakespeare's *Henry V*. Henry would die a few years later in France of dysentery at the age of thirty-five. His infant son, Henry VI, was crowned king of England and later crowned king of France in Paris. Henry VI would eventually lose both crowns.

RENCH ADVANCE

1 ounce gin
1 ounce blackberry liqueur
¾ ounce sweet vermouth
Splash grenadine
Splash Pernod

Add ice and water to a cocktail glass to chill the glass. Add ice to the tin side of a Boston shaker. In the mixing glass, add gin, blackberry liqueur, sweet vermouth, grenadine, and Pernod. Pour the contents of the mixing glass into the iced tin and secure the glass to the tin. Shake the contents until the ice sounds different and the contents are cold. Open the Boston shaker. Empty the cocktail glass, then strain the contents of the shaker into the empty glass. Serve.

Most people look at Hawaii as the fiftieth state in the United States, but until 1893, the chain of islands was the Kingdom of Hawaii. It was founded by King Kamehameha I "the Great" in 1795 and lasted until the reign of Queen Liliuokalani. The royal palace still exists and can be toured when visiting the island of Oahu—Hawaii is the only state in the United States that has a royal palace—and members of the royal family still live in Hawaii and other parts of the United States.

HAWAIIAN MARTINI

2 ounces gin
½ ounce triple sec
½ ounce pineapple juice

Add ice and water to a cocktail glass to chill the glass. Add ice to the tin side of a Boston shaker. In the mixing glass, add gin, triple sec, and pineapple juice. Pour the contents of the mixing glass into the iced tin and secure the glass to the tin. Shake the contents until the ice sounds different and the contents are cold. Open the Boston shaker. Empty the cocktail glass, then strain the contents of the shaker into the empty glass. Serve.

Imperial Germany was ruled by three kaisers, or emperors, and consisted of twenty-six member states, including four kingdoms and many duchies, grand duchies, and principalities. William I was the first emperor of Germany, followed by Frederick III, who only reigned for three months before passing away of cancer. He was succeeded by his son Wilhelm II. Fredrick III married Victoria, Princess Royal, the daughter of Queen Victoria and her consort, Prince Albert. During World War I, royal cousins Wilhelm II and George V fought in a dynastic civil war. After the Great War, all of the German dukes, grand dukes, and princes, not to mention the kaiser, lost their titles.

MPERIAL MARTINI

2 ounces gin
⅔ ounce dry vermouth
⅓ ounce maraschino liqueur

Add ice and water to a cocktail glass to chill the glass. Add ice to the tin side of a Boston shaker. In the mixing glass, add gin, dry vermouth, and maraschino liqueur. Pour the contents of the mixing glass into the iced tin and secure the glass to the tin. Shake the contents until the ice sounds different and the contents are cold. Open the Boston shaker. Empty the cocktail glass, then strain the contents of the shaker into the empty glass. Serve.

Lady Diana Spencer married Charles, Prince of Wales, in 1981. Over time, she became known as the People's Princess. She was the mother of Prince William, Duke of Cambridge, and Prince Harry, Duke of Sussex. Diana was the daughter of John Spencer, 8th Earl Spencer, and his first wife, the Hon. Frances Shand Kydd. Diana was known for her charity work, especially her work with HIV/AIDS patients. She died in 1997 in a car wreck in Paris, France, as she and the group she was traveling with were chased by paparazzi.

LADY DIANA

1½ ounces gin
1 ounce Campari
¾ ounce lime juice
½ ounce simple syrup

Add ice and water to a cocktail glass to chill the glass. Add ice to the tin side of a Boston shaker. In the mixing glass, add gin, Campari, lime juice, and simple syrup. Pour the contents of the mixing glass into the iced tin and secure the glass to the tin. Shake the contents until the ice sounds different and the contents are cold. Open the Boston shaker. Empty the cocktail glass, then strain the contents of the shaker into the empty glass. Serve.

Similar to Lady Diana, Georgiana Spencer was the daughter of an Earl Spencer, John Spencer, the person for whom the title was created. Lady Georgiana married William Cavendish, the 5th Duke of Devonshire. She was considered one of the most fashionable women of her time—a time when George III was on the throne and the Revolutionary War was waged in the American Colonies. Also, similar to her third great-grandniece, the duchess died before her time. Georgiana's story is detailed in the movie *The Duchess*, with Keira Knightley in the lead role.

$\mathcal{L}$ADY SCARLETT

1 ounce gin
1 ounce Cointreau
½ ounce lime juice
½ ounce dry vermouth
1 dash Angostura bitters

Add ice and water to a cocktail glass to chill the glass. Add ice to the tin side of a Boston shaker. In the mixing glass, add gin, Cointreau, lime juice, dry vermouth, and bitters. Pour the contents of the mixing glass into the iced tin and secure the glass to the tin. Shake the contents until the ice sounds different and the contents are cold. Open the Boston shaker. Empty the cocktail glass, then strain the contents of the shaker into the empty glass. Serve.

Many people consider themselves self-made, but few can claim that they are self-made emperors. Napoleon worked his way from being a commoner in Italy to ruler of the French empire, which included Italy, Spain, Switzerland, and Germany. After crowning himself, he ruled for about eleven years between 1804 and 1814 and for another short reign in 1815. He died at fifty-one as he began: a commoner.

NAPOLEON

2 ounces gin
½ ounce Grand Mariner
½ ounce Dubonnet Rouge

Add ice and water to a cocktail glass to chill the glass. Add ice to the tin side of a Boston shaker. In the mixing glass, add gin, Grand Mariner, and Dubonnet Rouge. Pour the contents of the mixing glass into the iced tin and secure the glass to the tin. Shake the contents until the ice sounds different and the contents are cold. Open the Boston shaker. Empty the cocktail glass, then strain the contents of the shaker into the empty glass. Serve.

The story of the negroni cocktail started after World War I, when Count Negroni wanted an Americano (vermouth and Campari) but with more punch. The bartender added gin instead of sparkling water. It is the perfect drink before dinner.

NEGRONI

1 ounce gin
1 ounce Campari
1 ounce sweet vermouth
Orange twist

Add ice to an old-fashioned glass. In the mixing glass, add ice then add gin, Campari, and sweet vermouth. Stir at least forty times. Strain into the old-fashioned glass. Add the orange twist and serve.

Beijing was once known as Peking and is home to the Forbidden City, the seat of power for the Chinese empire. The empire was several millennia old when the last emperor, Puyi, ruled. He was the 11th emperor of the Qing dynasty. Puyi came to the throne before his third birthday and lost the throne by forced abdication by the age of nine, before World War I. He tried several times to return to his former position. In 1967, he died at the age of sixty-one as a citizen of China.

 PEKING EXPRESS

1½ ounces gin
1 ounce Cointreau
½ ounce white crème de menthe
½ ounce egg white

Add ice and water to a cocktail glass to chill the glass. Add ice to the tin side of a Boston shaker. In the mixing glass, add gin, Cointreau, white crème de menthe, and egg white. Pour the contents of the mixing glass into the iced tin and secure the glass to the tin. Shake the contents until the ice sounds different and the contents are cold. Open the Boston shaker. Empty the cocktail glass, then strain the contents of the shaker into the empty glass. Serve. .

Prince William, Duke of Cambridge, is the first son of Charles, Prince of Wales, and Princess Diana. He is behind his father in line for the throne. In 2011, he married Catherine Middleton; together they have three children: Prince George, Princess Charlotte, and Prince Louis. Prince William is a Knight of the Garter and the Knight of the Thistle. Since he was a small boy, the prince has always had an infectious smile. He does have a lot to smile about.

Prince's Smile

1½ ounces gin
¾ ounce Calvados
¾ ounce apricot brandy
¼ ounce lemon juice

Add ice and water to a cocktail glass to chill the glass. Add ice to the tin side of a Boston shaker. In the mixing glass, add gin, Calvados, apricot brandy, and lemon juice. Pour the contents of the mixing glass into the iced tin and secure the glass to the tin. Shake the contents until the ice sounds different and the contents are cold. Open the Boston shaker. Empty the cocktail glass, then strain the contents of the shaker into the empty glass. Serve.

A change in Swedish law in 1979 moved Princess Victoria ahead of her younger brother, Prince Carl Phillip, in line for the throne. Victoria, Crown Princess of Sweden, Duchess of Västergötland, is married to Prince Daniel, and the couple has two children: Princess Estelle, Duchess of Östergötland, and Prince Oscar, Duke of Skåne. Sweden will most likely enjoy a queen as its next monarch.

PRINCESS MARTINI

1 ounce gin
1 ounce orange juice
1 ounce pineapple juice
½ ounce sparkling wine

Add ice and water to a cocktail glass to chill the glass. Add ice to the tin side of a Boston shaker. In the mixing glass, add gin, orange juice, and pineapple juice. Pour the contents of the mixing glass into the iced tin and secure the glass to the tin. Shake the contents until the ice sounds different and the contents are cold. Open the Boston shaker. Empty the cocktail glass, then strain the contents of the shaker into the empty glass. Top the cocktail with sparkling wine. Serve.

Queen Elizabeth I of England and Ireland was the last Tudor monarch. Elizabeth was the daughter of King Henry VIII and his second wife, Anne Boleyn. In 1558, she acceded to the throne at twenty-five and ruled for forty-five years, during which time she solidified the Church of England and defeated Spain. Even though she was pursued by many suitors, Elizabeth never married.

QUEEN ELIZABETH

2 ounces gin
¾ ounces dry vermouth
¼ ounce Bénédictine

Add ice and water to a cocktail glass to chill the glass. Add ice to the tin side of a Boston shaker. In the mixing glass, add gin, dry vermouth, and Bénédictine. Pour the contents of the mixing glass into the iced tin and secure the glass to the tin. Shake the contents until the ice sounds different and the contents are cold. Open the Boston shaker. Empty the cocktail glass, then strain the contents of the shaker into the empty glass. Serve.

Charles Spencer, 9th Earl Spencer, is the younger brother of Diana Princess of Wales. He has three children by three wives, including his heir, Louis Spencer, Viscount Althorp. The Earls Spencer date back to 1765, and the Earls are directly descended from the 1st Duke of Marlborough.

SPENCER COCKTAIL

1½ ounces gin
¾ ounce apricot brandy
½ ounce orange juice
1 dash orange bitters

Add ice and water to a cocktail glass to chill the glass. Add ice to the tin side of a Boston shaker. In the mixing glass, add gin, apricot brandy, orange juice, and bitters. Pour the contents of the mixing glass into the iced tin and secure the glass to the tin. Shake the contents until the ice sounds different and the contents are cold. Open the Boston shaker. Empty the cocktail glass, then strain the contents of the shaker into the empty glass. Serve.

The White Rose symbolized the House of York in the epic War of the Roses, a civil war between cousins for control of the English Throne. On the opposing side, the Red Rose was for the House of Lancaster.

HITE ROSE

1½ ounces gin
½ ounce lime juice
½ ounce maraschino liqueur
½ ounce orange juice
½ ounce egg white
¼ ounce simple syrup

Add ice and water to a cocktail glass to chill the glass. Add ice to the tin side of a Boston shaker. In the mixing glass, add simple syrup, egg white, orange juice, maraschino liqueur, lime juice, and gin. Pour the contents of the mixing glass into the iced tin and secure the glass to the tin. Shake the contents until the ice sounds different and the contents are cold. Open the Boston shaker. Empty the cocktail glass, then strain the contents of the shaker into the empty glass. Serve.

The Tudor rose, or the Union rose, combined the red rose of the House of Lancaster and the white rose from the House of York, showing the union after the civil war that is known as the War of the Roses.

$\mathcal{E}$NGLISH ROSE

1½ ounces dry gin
¾ ounce dry vermouth
¾ ounce apricot brandy
Splash grenadine

Add ice and water to a cocktail glass to chill the glass. Add ice to the tin side of a Boston shaker. In the mixing glass, add dry gin, dry vermouth, and apricot brandy. Pour the contents of the mixing glass into the iced tin and secure the glass to the tin. Shake the contents until the ice sounds different and the contents are cold. Open the Boston shaker. Empty the cocktail glass, then strain the contents of the shaker into the empty glass. Serve.

Three men have been declared monarch of Haiti. The three have much in common: each declared himself monarch, and each was removed from the throne. The first empire was declared by Jean-Jacques Dessalines as Emperor Jacques I. He ruled for about two years. A few years later, Henri Christopher declared himself King Henri. He ruled for less than ten years. Faustin-Elie Soulouque was crowned Emperor Faustin I and ruled for less than ten years. Each of these monarchs was replaced by a republic. Haiti is known for Haitian Vodou. One of the loa (spirit intermediaries) is Baron Samedi, who is the loa of the dead and the giver of life. Baron Samedi is usually well dressed and very fashionable.

BARON SAMEDI

1½ ounces dry gin
½ ounce cherry brandy
3 ounces ginger ale
2 ounces orange juice
Orange slice

Add ice to a Collins glass to chill the glass. Add the gin, cherry brandy, orange juice, and ginger ale to the glass. Stir and garnish with the orange slice. Serve.

The Smithsonian Institution in Washington, DC, holds the last remnant of a huge blue diamond of perfect clarity, the Tavernier Blue, that was once owned by Louis XIV of France. The original was roughly 115 carats. Shortly after he acquired the massive blue gem, the diamond was cut down to sixty-eight carats and named French Blue (Le Bleu de France). The diamond was stolen from the French crown jewels during the French Revolution, cut again to forty-five and a half carats, and renamed the Hope Diamond.

BLUE DIAMOND

¾ ounce gin
¾ ounce crème de violette
¼ ounce blue curaçao
Lemon wedge
3 ounces sparkling wine

Add ice and water to a champagne flute to chill the glass.
Add ice to the tin side of a Boston shaker. In the mixing glass,
add gin, crème de violette, blue curaçao, and the juice of the
lemon wedge. Pour the contents of the mixing glass into the
iced tin and secure the glass to the tin. Shake the contents
until the ice sounds different and the contents are cold. Open
the Boston shaker. Empty the champagne flute, then strain
the contents of the shaker into the empty glass. Top the
cocktail with sparkling wine. Serve.

The current line of the Earl of Suffolk dates back to 1603, when Thomas Howard was honored with the title by King James I and VI. The title has passed down from father to son to the current title holder, Michael Howard, 21st Earl of Suffolk, who is also the 14th Earl of Berkshire.

$\mathscr{L}$ORD SUFFOLK COCKTAIL

2 ounces London dry gin
½ ounce sweet vermouth
½ ounce maraschino liqueur

Add ice and water to a cocktail glass to chill the glass. Add
ice to the tin side of a Boston shaker. In the mixing glass,
add gin, sweet vermouth, and maraschino liqueur. Pour
the contents of the mixing glass into the iced tin and secure
the glass to the tin. Shake the contents until the ice sounds
different and the contents are cold. Open the Boston shaker.
Empty the champagne flute, then strain the contents of the
shaker into the empty glass. Top the cocktail with sparkling
wine. Serve.

The Order of the Red Lion and the Sun was established during the reign of the last Shah of Iran (1941–1979) to honor those who saved lives or rendered humanitarian services to the Iranian people.

ED LION

1 ounce gin
1½ ounces Cointreau
¼ ounce orange juice
¼ ounce lemon juice
Lemon twist

Add ice and water to a cocktail glass to chill the glass. Add ice to the tin side of a Boston shaker. In the mixing glass, add gin, Cointreau, orange juice, and lemon juice. Pour the contents of the mixing glass into the iced tin and secure the glass to the tin. Shake the contents until the ice sounds different and the contents are cold. Open the Boston shaker. Empty the cocktail glass, then strain the contents of the shaker into the empty glass. Garnish with lemon twist. Serve.

The saying "The sun never sets on the British empire" refers to the sun always being in the sky in some part of the British holdings around the world. Part of the success of the British colonialism included an army and a navy that was able to occupy various counties. This exposed the soldiers to various deadly diseases. Quinine was the key to keeping many of the soldiers and sailors healthy. The quinine was added to sparkling water, producing tonic water. Tonic pairs well with gin, so we have the gin and tonic.

IN AND TONIC

2 ounces gin
4 ounces tonic water
2 slices of lime

Add ice to an old-fashioned glass. Then add the gin and top with tonic water. The carbonated tonic water will mix the drink. Garnish with lime. Serve.

Prince George, Duke of Kent, was the fourth son of King George V and his consort, Queen Mary, and brother to both King Edward VIII and King George VI. During World War II, he was killed in a military air crash at the age of thirty-nine. He is one of a very few members of the royal family who died during active military service in centuries. His six-year-old son, Prince Edward, succeeded him as the Duke of Kent and still holds the title today.

VIATION

2 ounces gin
½ ounce maraschino liqueur

½ ounce lemon juice
Cocktail cherry

Add ice and water to a cocktail glass to chill the glass. Add ice to a cocktail shaker. Add the lemon juice, maraschino liqueur, and gin to the cocktail shaker. Shake until you hear the ice change and the drink is cold. Empty the glass and strain the cocktail into the glass. Garnish with the cocktail cherry.

RUM COCKTAILS

Rum is made all over the world from sugar, sugar cane juice, molasses, or other sugar by-products. Rum is another bartender favorite because of the spirit's flexibility in cocktails. Rum comes in a wide spectrum of clear to brown colors based on how long the rum ages in oak barrels that have been burned on the inside. Most are distilled to a high proof and watered down to a market 80 proof (40% alcohol by volume). Some rum is sold at a higher "overproof" 151 proof (75.5% alcohol by volume).

Queen Alexandra of Denmark was the consort to King Edward VII. Her father was Christian IX, King of Denmark, and her brother was the Greek choice to become King of the Hellenes as George I. Alexandra and Edward had six children, including two who would become monarchs: George V of Britain and Maud, Queen of Norway.

ALEXANDRA

1 ounce coffee liqueur
1 ounce rum
1 ounce coconut cream
1 ounce cream
Cocktail cherry

Add ice to a Collins glass. Add the coffee liqueur, rum, coconut cream, and cream to the Collins glass and stir. Garnish with cocktail cherry. Serve.

A high horse is important for a monarch to review troops and for parades. This tradition comes from a time when monarchs were on the battlefield. Riding a horse gives the viewer a distinct advantage over standing on the ground. This practice has led to the phrase, "Get off your high horse," which means that someone is being arrogant.

High Horse Cocktail

1½ ounces aged rum
½ ounce kirsch brandy
½ ounce cherry liqueur
½ ounce sweet vermouth
2 dashes Angostura bitters
Cocktail cherry

Add ice and water to a cocktail glass to chill the glass. In the mixing glass, add aged rum, kirsch brandy, cherry liqueur, sweet vermouth, and Angostura bitters. Stir the contents thirty to forty times until the contents are cold. Empty the cocktail glass, then strain the contents of the shaker into the empty glass. Garnish with a cocktail cherry. Serve.

An ambassador is a diplomat of the highest order. A monarch can rely on the ambassador to convey messages to other monarchs or heads of state with the goal of keeping peace between two countries.

MBASSADOR

2 ounces rum
1 ounce sweet and sour mix
3 ounces ginger beer
Lime twist

Add ice to an old-fashioned glass. Add the rum, sweet and sour mix, and the ginger beer. Garnish with a lime twist. Serve.

Cleopatra of Egypt was queen of the Ptolemaic Kingdom and lover to both Julius Caesar and Mark Antony. She was the mother of Caesarion, Caesar's son, the last Pharaoh of Egypt, and Ptolemy Philadelphus, Antony's son, King of Syria.

CLEOPATRA

2 ounces rum
1 ounce sweet and sour mix
½ ounce amaretto
3 dashes Angostura bitters
Lemon twist

Add ice and water to a cocktail glass to chill the glass. Add ice to the tin side of a Boston shaker. In the mixing glass, add the rum, sweet and sour mix, amaretto, and Angostura bitters. Pour the contents of the mixing glass into the iced tin and secure the glass to the tin. Shake the contents until the ice sounds different and the contents are cold. Open the

Boston shaker. Empty the cocktail glass, then strain the contents of the shaker into the empty glass. Garnish with a lemon twist. Serve.

When you live a royal life in a palace, you always need to worry about security. Queen Elizabeth II experienced a close call on July 9, 1982, when someone climbed the fourteen-foot walls outside Buckingham Palace, broke into the palace, and found his way to the monarch's bedroom, where the queen was sleeping. He woke the queen, and she called for help. The fence jumper was arrested.

FENCE JUMPER

¾ ounce rum
¾ ounce tequila
2 dashes Tabasco

Prepare a shot glass. Add the rum and tequila then top with Tabasco. Serve.

Early in 1893, the United States assisted in the overthrow of the Hawaiian monarchy, ending Queen Liliuokalani's reign. The royal forces of fewer than five hundred soldiers were overwhelmed by the revolutionary army with reinforcements from the United States Navy and Marines. The kingdom was converted into a republic and five years later annexed into the United States.

AWAIIAN SCREW

1 ounce rum
1 ounce vodka
2 ounces orange juice
2 ounces pineapple juice

Add ice to an old-fashioned glass. Add ice to the tin side of a Boston shaker. In the mixing glass, add the rum, vodka, orange juice, and pineapple juice. Pour the contents of the mixing glass into the iced tin and secure the glass to the tin. Shake the contents until the ice sounds different and the contents are cold. Open the Boston shaker. Strain the contents of the shaker into the ice-filled glass. Serve.

Many countries in the British Commonwealth are ruled by the British monarch. Jamaica is one of them. When visiting Jamaica, the queen is first referred to as the Queen of Jamaica. She is the first monarch to hold that specific title.

AMAICAN

1 ounce rum
1 ounce coffee liqueur
1 ounce sweet and sour mix
3 ounces club soda
1 dash Angostura bitters

Add ice to a highball glass. Add ice to the tin side of a Boston shaker. In the mixing glass, add rum, coffee liqueur, sweet and sour mix, and Angostura bitters. Pour the contents of the mixing glass into the iced tin and secure the glass to the tin. Shake the contents until the ice sounds different and the contents are cold. Open the Boston shaker. Strain the contents of the shaker into the empty glass. Serve.

King Albert I of the Belgians was a hero for Belgium during World War I. Kaiser Wilhelm II wrote his cousin Albert to let him know that the German Army would cut through Belgium on their way to France. Albert wrote back telling the German emperor not to cross the shared Belgian border. The German invading force was ten times the size of the entire Belgian Army. With King Albert at the head of the army throughout the war, the Belgians resisted the German invasion and saved Belgium. Albert was part of the Saxe-Coburg and Gotha House. In a similar move to the British, Albert changed the house name to the House of Belgium after World War I. Albert enjoyed mountaineering. He died in a solo rock-climbing accident in in 1934. Albert's great-grandson, King Philippe of the Belgians, took the oath of office on July 21, 2013.

OUNTAINEER

1½ ounces rum
1 ounce orange juice
½ ounce ginger ale
¼ ounce milk
¼ ounce lemon juice
Dash black pepper

Add ice to a Collins glass. Then add rum, orange juice, ginger ale, milk, and lemon juice. Stir and garnish with a dash of pepper. Serve.

The Saxon House of Wessex started with Cerdic, King of Wessex, in 519 and lasted off and on until Edward the Confessor, who died in January 1066. Saxon rule ended with the Norman invasion led by King William the Conqueror.

$\mathcal{S}$AXON

2 ounces rum
¼ ounce lime juice
¼ ounce grenadine

Add ice and water to a cocktail glass to chill the glass. Add ice to the tin side of a Boston shaker. In the mixing glass, add rum, lime juice, and grenadine. Pour the contents of the mixing glass into the iced tin and secure the glass to the tin. Shake the contents until the ice sounds different and the contents are cold. Open the Boston shaker. Empty the cocktail glass, then strain the contents of the shaker into the empty glass. Serve.

King Pōmare founded the Kingdom of Tahiti in 1788. The Pacific island kingdom lasted until the French took the island and forced King Pōmare V to abdicate in 1880. His descendants continue to press their claims.

AHITIAN TEA

1 ounce rum
¾ ounce vodka
¾ ounce gin
¾ ounce triple sec
4 ounces orange juice

Add ice to a hurricane glass. Add ice to the tin side of a Boston shaker. In the mixing glass, add rum, vodka, gin, and triple sec. Pour the contents of the mixing glass into the iced tin and secure the glass to the tin. Shake the contents until the ice sounds different and the contents are cold. Open the Boston shaker. Strain the contents of the shaker into the ice-filled glass. Serve.

King Richard III was the last Plantagenet king and the last king from the House of York. He claimed the throne after his preteen nephews, Edward V and Richard, Duke of York, disappeared in 1483. Richard III was killed less than two years later in the Battle of Bosworth Field. The remains of the boys and their uncle were lost for a time after their deaths. The boys' skeletons may have been found in the Tower of London. Their uncle's body was found in the remains of Greyfriars Church in Leicester.

RAVE DIGGER

¾ ounce 151-proof rum
¾ ounce bourbon

Prepare a shot glass. Add ice to the tin side of a Boston shaker. In the mixing glass, add the overproof rum and the bourbon. Pour the contents of the mixing glass into the iced tin and secure the glass to the tin. Shake the contents until the ice sounds different and the contents are cold. Open the Boston shaker. Strain the contents of the shaker into the empty shot glass. Serve.

Cardinal Armand Jean du Plessis, Duke of Richelieu and Fronsac, was a power broker during the reign of King Louis XIII, serving as a close advisor to the king throughout his tenure.

ARDINAL

1½ ounces aged rum
½ ounce maraschino liqueur
¼ ounce triple sec
¼ ounce grenadine
Cocktail cherry

Add ice and water to a cocktail glass to chill the glass. Add ice to the tin side of a Boston shaker. In the mixing glass, add rum, maraschino liqueur, triple sec, and grenadine. Pour the contents of the mixing glass into the iced tin and secure the glass to the tin. Shake the contents until the ice sounds different and the contents are cold. Open the Boston shaker. Empty the cocktail glass, then strain the contents of the shaker into the empty glass. Garnish with a cocktail cherry. Serve.

For those who can't travel to see a magical royal house, one exists at Disney. The Disney Castle is a distinct symbol that is part of the Disney brand. For those looking to Florida, the mailing address is in the town of Lake Buena Vista.

$\mathscr{B}$UENA VISTA

¾ ounce dark rum
¾ ounce grenadine
½ ounce sweet vermouth
½ ounce sweetened lime juice
Lemon twist
Cocktail cherry

Add ice and water to a cocktail glass to chill the glass. Add ice to the tin side of a Boston shaker. In the mixing glass, add dark rum, grenadine, sweet vermouth, and sweetened lime juice. Pour the contents of the mixing glass into the iced tin and secure the glass to the tin. Shake the contents until the ice sounds different and the contents are cold. Open the Boston shaker. Empty the cocktail glass, then strain the contents of the shaker into the empty glass. Garnish with lemon twist and cocktail cherry. Serve.

King George VI had issues speaking in public. When his brother Edward VIII abdicated, that pushed George into a role that required good speaking skills. The story is dramatized in the 2010 award-winning movie *The King's Speech*, starring Colin Firth as King George VI, Helena Bonham Carter as Queen Elizabeth the Queen Mother, and Geoffrey Rush as Lionel Logue, the king's speech therapist. Logue received

Commander in the Royal Victorian Order for his services to the crown. The king worked hard on his speech issue and became the ruler and communicator Britain needed during World War II.

OMMUNICATOR

1½ ounces dark rum
½ ounce Galliano
¼ ounce crème de cacao

Add ice to an old-fashioned glass. Add dark rum, Galliano, and crème de cacao, and then stir. Serve.

Queen Elizabeth the Queen Mother learned to shoot in Buckingham Palace garden in case the Nazis tried to kidnap the royal family. The bombs dropped on London helped to provide targets. The bombs displaced many rats, so Queen Elizabeth would use the rats for target practice.

UNFIRE

1 ounce dark rum
5 ounces hot tea

Add the dark rum to a coffee cup, then top with hot tea. Serve.

King James I of Scotland was still a prince when he was sent away to France. The ship he was on was captured by a pirate ship, whose crew discovered the young prince. The pirates took James to the court of King Henry IV of England. When word reached the court that James's father, King Robert III, had died, the English king educated and helped James transition to from prince to king. King James would stay at the English court through the reigns of Henry IV and Henry V. James took part in the Hundred Years' War, fighting for the English, and was knighted by Henry V. When Henry V died, the English court started negotiations with the Scottish court to return James to his kingdom.

OLLY ROGER

1 ounce dark rum
1 ounce crème de banana
2 ounces lemon juice

Add ice and water to a cocktail glass to chill the glass. Add ice to the tin side of a Boston shaker. In the mixing glass, add dark rum, crème de banana, and lemon juice. Pour the contents of the mixing glass into the iced tin and secure the glass to the tin. Shake the contents until the ice sounds different and the contents are cold. Open the Boston shaker. Strain the contents of the shaker into the empty glass. Serve.

The last crown princess of the Kingdom of Hawaii was Victoria Kawekiu Ka'iulani Lunalilo Kalaninuiahilapalapa Cleghorn. She was more commonly known as Princess Ka'iulani. She was named for Queen Victoria and spent time in Britain.

After the overthrow of the monarchy, she died at the young age of twenty-three.

RINCESS

1 ounce dark rum
1 ounce crème de banana
1 ounce lemon juice

Add ice and water to a cocktail glass to chill the glass. Add ice to the tin side of a Boston shaker. In the mixing glass, add dark rum, crème de banana, and lemon juice. Pour the contents of the mixing glass into the iced tin and secure the glass to the tin. Shake the contents until the ice sounds different and the contents are cold. Open the Boston shaker. Empty the cocktail glass, then strain the contents of the shaker into the empty glass. Serve.

If the Hawaiian Kingdom had survived, there is a good chance that the current king would be Quentin Kawānanakoa. In the late 1990s, he served as a member of the Hawaii House of Representatives.

UENTIN

1½ ounces dark rum
½ ounce coffee liqueur
1 ounce cream
Freshly ground nutmeg

Add ice and water to a cocktail glass to chill the glass. Add ice to the tin side of a Boston shaker. In the mixing glass, add dark rum, coffee liqueur, and cream. Pour the contents of the mixing glass into the iced tin and secure the glass to the tin. Shake the contents until the ice sounds different and the contents are cold. Open the Boston shaker. Empty the cocktail glass, then strain the contents of the shaker into the empty glass. Garnish with freshly ground nutmeg. Serve.

King Kamehameha I, or Kamehameha the Great, was the first monarch of the Kingdom of Hawaii.

KAMEHAMEHA RUM PUNCH

1 ounce light rum
½ ounce dark rum
½ ounce blackberry liqueur
½ ounce amaretto
1 ounce lime juice
3 ounces pineapple juice

Add ice to a highball glass. Add ice to the tin side of a Boston shaker. In the mixing glass, add light rum, dark rum, blackberry liqueur, amaretto, lime juice, and pineapple juice. Pour the contents of the mixing glass into the iced tin and secure the glass to the tin. Shake the contents until the ice sounds different and the contents are cold. Open the Boston shaker. Strain the contents of the shaker into the ice-filled glass. Serve.

Count Maximilian Karl Lamoral O'Donnell saved Emperor Franz Josef I of Austria when the emperor was attacked by a knife-wielding assassin. O'Donnell was already a German count, but the emperor honored him with knighthood and as a count of the Austrian empire.

IFESAVER

1 ounce light rum
1 ounce pineapple juice
¼ ounce lime juice
Splash blue curaçao
Splash triple sec
Splash simple syrup

Add ice and water to a cocktail glass to chill the glass. Add ice to the tin side of a Boston shaker. In the mixing glass, add rum, pineapple juice, lime juice, blue curaçao, triple sec, and simple syrup. Pour the contents of the mixing glass into the iced tin and secure the glass to the tin. Shake the contents until the ice sounds different and the contents are cold. Open the Boston shaker. Empty the cocktail glass, then strain the contents of the shaker into the empty glass. Serve.

The Spanish Navy is a historical powerhouse. The list of victories is long and dates from the 1200s to the modern era.

# NAVY COCKTAIL

1½ ounces light rum
1 ounce orange juice
1 ounce dry vermouth
Orange twist

Add ice and water to a cocktail glass to chill the glass. Add ice to the tin side of a Boston shaker. In the mixing glass, add light rum, orange juice, and dry vermouth. Pour the contents of the mixing glass into the iced tin and secure the glass to the tin. Shake the contents until the ice sounds different and the contents are cold. Open the Boston shaker. Empty the cocktail glass, then strain the contents of the shaker into the empty glass. Garnish with the orange twist. Serve.

The British Royal Navy has a reputation equal with the best in the world. Part of their success has been the ability to keep their sailors healthy. Admiral Edward Vernon helped with that during his time in the Royal Navy. Grog, or watered-down rum, may have been his invention. The name Grog comes from *grogram*, a cloth that he used for his coats. His sailors called him Old Grog.

# NAVY GROG

½ ounce light rum
½ ounce dark rum
½ ounce spiced rum
½ ounce orange juice

1 ounce pineapple juice
½ ounce guava juice
½ ounce lime juice
Orange slice

Add ice to a highball glass. Add ice to the tin side of a Boston shaker. In the mixing glass, add light rum, dark rum, spiced rum, orange juice, pineapple juice, guava juice, and lime juice. Pour the contents of the mixing glass into the iced tin and secure the glass to the tin. Shake the contents until the ice sounds different and the contents are cold. Open the Boston shaker. Strain the contents of the shaker into the ice-filled glass. Garnish with orange slice. Serve.

───────────────────────────────

Most monarchs would be thrilled to be an emperor. Most would not dream of becoming an emperor twice. Francis II and I was able to double his titles. He ruled as Francis II, Holy Roman Emperor from 1792 to 1806. In 1804, he took the title of emperor of Austria as Francis I and reigned until his death in 1835. The Order of the White Lion was inspired by Francis I and is the highest award of the Czech Republic.

$\mathcal{W}$HITE LION COCKTAIL

1½ ounces light rum
½ ounce lemon juice
Splash grenadine
Splash simple syrup
½ ounce egg white
2 dashes Angostura bitters

Add ice and water to a cocktail glass to chill the glass. Add ice to the tin side of a Boston shaker. In the mixing glass, add light rum, lemon juice, grenadine, simple syrup, egg white, and Angostura bitters. Pour the contents of the mixing glass into the iced tin and secure the glass to the tin. Shake the contents until the ice sounds different and the contents are cold. Open the Boston shaker. Empty the cocktail glass, then strain the contents of the shaker into the empty glass. Serve.

The beautiful island nation of St. Lucia is part of the British Commonwealth. Queen Elizabeth II is the monarch, and her title is Queen of St. Lucia.

T. LUCIA

2 ounces rum (white or golden)
1 ounce dry vermouth
1 ounce triple sec or curaçao

2 ounces orange juice
1 teaspoon grenadine
Cocktail cherry
Orange twist

Add ice and water to a highball glass to chill the glass. Add ice to the tin side of a Boston shaker. In the mixing glass, add the rum, vermouth, triple sec or curaçao, orange juice, and grenadine. Pour the contents of the mixing glass into the iced tin and secure the glass to the tin. Shake the contents until the ice sounds different and the contents are cold. Open the Boston shaker. Empty the highball glass, then refill with ice and strain the contents of the shaker into the glass. Garnish with orange twist and cocktail cherry. Serve.

TEQUILA AND MESCAL COCKTAILS

Tequila and mescal are both made from the agave plant. The agave plant takes eight to twelve years to reach maturity, which means tequila makers must project a decade in advance the demand for tequila. Like rum, tequila is aged to varying degrees in burned oak barrels, many of them being used bourbon and cognac barrels. As the tequila ages, the charred barrels lend more color to the spirit. Blanco or plata is tequila that is aged less than two months in stainless steel or neutral oak barrels. Joven or oro is generally unaged tequila that is flavored with caramel coloring. Reposado is tequila that is aged a minimum of two months but less than a year in oak barrels. Añejo is tequila that is aged for a minimum of a year but less than three years in oak barrels. Finally, extra añejo is aged for a minimum of three years in oak barrels. The longer tequila is aged, the darker the liquid becomes and the more influence the wood has on the flavor. The longer tequila is aged, the higher the price of the tequila. Cocktails rarely call for the pricy long-aged tequilas.

The Battle of Camlann is the final battle in which King Arthur died or was wounded and where Sir Mordred was killed. Some say that King Arthur was delivered to Avalon, where Morgan le Fay healed him, and that King Arthur will one day return.

ARTURO'S DEATH

1 ounce tequila
½ ounce rum
½ ounce vodka

½ ounce sweet vermouth
½ ounce Cointreau
Lemon twist

Add ice to the tin side of a Boston shaker. In the mixing glass, add the tequila, rum, vodka, sweet vermouth, and Cointreau. Pour the contents of the mixing glass into the iced tin and secure the glass to the tin. Shake the contents until the ice sounds different and the contents are cold. Open the Boston shaker. Strain the contents of the shaker into an empty highball glass, then fill with crushed ice. Garnish with a lemon twist. Serve.

When royalty travels in an official capacity and arrives at a new location, they are usually met with a brass band. The band usually plays the country's national or royal anthem.

$\mathcal{B}$RASS

1½ ounces tequila
1½ ounces passion fruit liqueur

Add ice and water to a cocktail glass to chill the glass. Add ice to the tin side of a Boston shaker. In the mixing glass, add tequila and passion fruit liqueur. Pour the contents of the mixing glass into the iced tin and secure the glass to the tin. Shake the contents until the ice sounds different and the contents are cold. Open the Boston shaker. Empty the cocktail glass, then strain the contents of the shaker into the empty glass. Serve.

King Charles II's father, King Charles I, was executed at the end of an English civil war. England entered an interregnum with Oliver Cromwell as the Lord Protector. When Cromwell died, the English invited Charles II back as king; this period of time was known as the Restoration. The 1995 Academy Award–winning film *Restoration* starred Robert Downey Jr., Meg Ryan, Hugh Grant, and Sam Neill as the restored monarch. Both the movie and Charles's reign featured the Great Plague that killed many Londoners. Charles II fathered many children, including many illegitimate children. Some of the illegitimate children were granted titles. Some of these titles survive, including the Duke of Buccleuch, the Duke of Grafton, the Duke of St. Albans, and the Duke of Richmond. Ironically, for these titles to survive all the heirs, from the sons of the 1st Dukes to now, have been required to be legitimate sons.

 # BLACK DEATH

¾ ounce tequila
¾ ounce bourbon

Prepare a shot glass. Add ice to the tin side of a Boston shaker. In the mixing glass, add tequila and bourbon. Pour the contents of the mixing glass into the iced tin and secure the glass to the tin. Shake the contents until the ice sounds different and the contents are cold. Open the Boston shaker. Strain the contents of the shaker into the empty glass. Serve.

Mexico has experienced two emperors. The first emperor was Mexican General Agustin I, who lasted less than a year as monarch. The second emperor was Maximillian I, an Austrian archduke and brother to Austrian Emperor Franz Joseph I. The French-backed Maximillian I reigned for three years before he was overthrown and executed. Cinco de Mayo celebrates the outcome of the Battle of Puebla, the Mexican victory over the French forces of Emperor Napoleon III, which happened before the Second Mexican Empire.

INCO DE MAYO

1½ ounces tequila
¾ ounce sweetened lime juice
¾ ounce grenadine
Lime twist

Add ice and water to a cocktail glass to chill the glass. Add ice to the tin side of a Boston shaker. In the mixing glass, add tequila, sweetened lime juice, and grenadine. Pour the contents of the mixing glass into the iced tin and secure the glass to the tin. Shake the contents until the ice sounds different and the contents are cold. Open the Boston shaker. Empty the cocktail glass, then strain the contents of the shaker into the empty glass. Garnish with a lime twist. Serve.

Horatio Nelson, 1st Viscount Nelson, Duke of Bronté, was a vice admiral in the British Royal Navy. Nelson came from humble beginnings; his father was an Anglican priest. But Nelson was able to rise through the ranks, and his talent was awarded with noble titles, including Baron Nelson and Viscount Nelson, both in the United Kingdom, and Duke of Bronté in the Kingdom of Sicily. Nelson died without children, so some of the titles became extinct. However, Baron Nelson and Duke of Bronté passed to his elder brother, William Nelson, who was elevated to Earl Nelson and Viscount

Merton. After William, the title Duke of Bronté followed one line in the family, while the other titles followed another. The current Duke of Bronté is Alexander Hood, 4th Viscount Bridport, while Simon Nelson is the 10th Earl Nelson.

RAPESHOT

1½ ounces tequila
1 ounce grape juice
½ ounce Cointreau

Add ice and water to a cocktail glass to chill the glass. Add ice to the tin side of a Boston shaker. In the mixing glass, add tequila, grape juice, and Cointreau. Pour the contents of the mixing glass into the iced tin and secure the glass to the tin. Shake the contents until the ice sounds different and the contents are cold. Open the Boston shaker. Empty the cocktail glass, then strain the contents of the shaker into the empty glass. Serve.

Sometimes monarchies end because of guerilla actions. The Irish ended the British monarchy in Ireland and formed a republic. The Greeks ended their monarchy. The Spanish monarchy ended when Francisco Franco took over the country as caudillo (dictator), but the monarchy returned with King Juan Carlos I.

GUERILLA

1½ ounces tequila
¾ ounce Cointreau
2 dashes Bad Dog Fire and Damnation Bitters
Orange twist

Add ice and water to a cocktail glass to chill the glass. Add ice to the tin side of a Boston shaker. In the mixing glass, add tequila, Cointreau, and Bad Dog Fire and Damnation Bitters. Pour the contents of the mixing glass into the iced tin and secure the glass to the tin. Shake the contents until the ice sounds different and the contents are cold. Open the Boston shaker. Empty the cocktail glass, then strain the contents of the shaker into the empty glass. Garnish with the orange twist. Serve.

Cuauhtémoc was the last Aztec emperor. The Spanish had already invaded when he started his reign. The Spanish conquistador Hernán Cortés, Marquis of the Valley of Oaxaca, executed Cuauhtémoc.

MEXICAN HOT CHOCOLATE

1½ ounces tequila
½ ounce coffee liqueur
2 ounces cream
3 ounces hot chocolate

Prepare a large coffee cup with hot water to warm the cup. Once the cup is hot, empty the hot water. Pour the tequila in the cup followed by the coffee liqueur, cream, and hot chocolate. Stir and serve.

Montezuma II was one of the last rulers of the Aztec empire. During his reign, the empire reached its zenith. He lost his life at the hands of the Spanish conquistadors led by Hernán Cortés.

ONTEZUMA

1½ ounces tequila
1 ounce Madeira
1 egg yolk (or 1 ounce of pasteurized egg yolk)
3 ice cubes

Add ice and water to a champagne flute to chill the glass. Add the tequila, Madeira, egg yolk, and ice to a blender. Empty the champagne flute, then strain the contents of the shaker into the empty glass. Serve.

During World War I, many armor-piercing shells filled with TNT were used to maximize damage. These were used by both the Royal Army and Navy of Britain and the Imperial forces of Germany.

NT

1½ ounces tequila
4 ounces tonic water
Lemon twist

Add ice to a highball glass. Add the tequila to the highball glass and fill with tonic water. Garnish with a lemon twist. Serve.

Drinking before battle or during a battle is as old as battles. The liquid courage was used even with the earliest alcoholic beverages. Gin was referred to as Dutch courage, and knights were said to "pay for their mead" the day of battle from the beverages they consumed the night before the battle.

WARRIOR'S CUP

1 ounce tequila
1 ounce amaretto
½ ounce Scotch whisky
Orange twist

Add ice to an old-fashioned glass, then add the tequila, amaretto, and Scotch whisky. Garnish with an orange twist. Serve.

Every year the Royal Swedish Academy of Sciences, Swedish Academy, and the Norwegian Noble Committee award Nobel Prizes. The prizes are named for Alfred Nobel, who invented many things but is best known for his explosive inventions. He left most of his fortune to establish awards that would honor discoveries that would benefit humankind.

XPLOSIVE

1 ounce reposado tequila
½ ounce Cointreau

Prepare a shot glass. Add ice to the tin side of a Boston shaker. In the mixing glass, add reposado tequila and Cointreau. Pour the contents of the mixing glass into the iced tin and secure the glass to the tin. Shake the contents until the ice sounds different and the contents are cold. Open the Boston shaker. Strain the contents of the shaker into the empty shot glass. Serve.

King Robert the Bruce is known for helping to reestablish an independent Kingdom of Scotland. The Bruce killed a cousin in the church of the Greyfriars at Dumfries to claim the throne. This created a mess for the future king. He was excommunicated by the pope. Robert claimed the throne in 1306, but this claim was not recognized by the pope until 1324. Many battles were fought in the interim, and many lives were lost on both sides. Robert died in 1329.

LOODBATH

¾ ounce tequila
¾ ounce strawberry liqueur

Prepare a shot glass. Add ice to the tin side of a Boston shaker. In the mixing glass, add tequila and strawberry liqueur. Pour the contents of the mixing glass into the iced tin and secure the glass to the tin. Shake the contents until the ice sounds different and the contents are cold. Open the Boston shaker. Strain the contents of the shaker into the empty shot glass. Serve.

India's move toward independence took many years of negotiation. Lord Louis Mountbatten was the last viceroy (1947) and first governor-general (1947–1948) of India. Lord Mountbatten assisted India in gaining independence.

MPIRE STRIKES BACK

1½ ounces tequila
⅓ ounce vanilla liqueur
½ ounce passion fruit juice
½ ounce cream

Add ice and water to a cocktail glass to chill the glass. Add ice to the tin side of a Boston shaker. In the mixing glass, add tequila, vanilla liqueur, passion fruit juice, and cream. Pour the contents of the mixing glass into the iced tin and secure the glass to the tin. Shake the contents until the ice sounds

different and the contents are cold. Open the Boston shaker.
Empty the cocktail glass, then strain the contents of the
shaker into the empty glass. Serve.

The French colonial empire has existed twice—first from 1804 to 1814 (with a short period in 1815) and second from 1852 to 1870. It rivaled the British empire; however, the sun would set on this empire.

 FRENCH MARGARITA

1 ounce tequila
1 ounce blood orange juice
½ ounce Cointreau
⅓ ounce lime juice
¼ ounce agave syrup

Add ice and water to a cocktail glass or margarita glass to chill the glass. Add ice to the tin side of a Boston shaker. In the mixing glass, add tequila, blood orange juice, Cointreau, lime juice, and agave syrup. Pour the contents of the mixing glass into the iced tin and secure the glass to the tin. Shake the contents until the ice sounds different and the contents are cold. Open the Boston shaker. Empty the cocktail glass, then strain the contents of the shaker into the empty glass. Serve.

Prince Henry, Duke of Gloucester, was born in 1900, the third son of King George V and his consort, Queen Mary. He was the younger brother of King Edward VIII and King

George VI. Prince Henry served in the army. Near the end of World War II, in 1944, he was promoted to general, and by 1955, he had been promoted to field marshal. He served as governor-general of Australia from 1945 to 1947.

GENERAL'S SALUTE

1½ ounces tequila
½ ounce Cointreau
¼ ounce simple syrup
4 ice cubes

Add ice and water to a cocktail glass to chill the glass. Add the ice, tequila, Cointreau, and simple syrup to a blender. Blend until smooth. Empty the cocktail glass, then strain the contents of the shaker into the empty glass. Serve.

Princess Grace Kelly was an American actress until she met Prince Rainier III of Monaco. Kelly won an Academy Award for Best Actress in 1954. The next year, she met Prince Rainier. They married in 1956 and had three children: Princess Caroline, Prince Albert, and Princess Stephanie. Princess Grace died in 1982.

GRACE OF MONACO

1 ounce tequila
1 ounce apricot brandy
1 ounce Mandarine Napoléon
Orange twist

Add ice to an old-fashioned glass to chill the glass. Add ice to the tin side of a Boston shaker. In the mixing glass, add tequila, apricot brandy, and Mandarine Napoléon. Pour the contents of the mixing glass into the iced tin and secure the glass to the tin. Shake the contents until the ice sounds different and the contents are cold. Open the Boston shaker. Strain the contents of the shaker into the ice-filled glass. Garnish with an orange twist. Serve.

Prince Felix Yusupov was a member of the Russian royal family who helped to assassinate Grigori Rasputin in 1916, near the end of the Russian monarchy. The prince and his wife were exiled and lived in Paris for the rest of their lives.

# Monk's Man

1½ ounces tequila
1½ ounces Frangelico

Add ice to an old-fashioned glass. Add ice to the tin side of a Boston shaker. In the mixing glass, add tequila and Frangelico. Pour the contents of the mixing glass into the iced tin and secure the glass to the tin. Shake the contents until the ice sounds different and the contents are cold. Open the Boston shaker. Strain the contents of the shaker into the empty glass. Serve.

King Ludwig II of Bavaria succeeded to the throne at eighteen in 1864. In his twenty-two-year reign, he built some amazing castles, including Neuschwanstein Castle. Some claim that

Ludwig was insane, and eventually this may have caught up with him. He was found dead in waist-deep water.

LEADING INSANITY

½ ounce tequila
½ ounce vodka
½ ounce dark rum

Prepare a shot glass. Add ice to the tin side of a Boston shaker. In the mixing glass, add tequila, vodka, and dark rum. Pour the contents of the mixing glass into the iced tin and secure the glass to the tin. Shake the contents until the ice sounds different and the contents are cold. Open the Boston shaker. Strain the contents of the shaker into the empty shot glass. Serve.

The island of Iona in Scotland is a home to an ancient abbey/monastery and a royal graveyard. Some of the former kings that are in the graveyard include Kenneth I, Malcolm I, Duncan I, and Macbeth.

KELETON

1½ ounces tequila
2 ounces blackberry juice
2 ounces lemon-lime soda
Lime twist

Add ice to a highball. Add ice to the tin side of a Boston shaker. In the mixing glass, add tequila and blackberry juice. Pour the contents of the mixing glass into the iced tin and secure the glass to the tin. Shake the contents until the ice sounds different and the contents are cold. Open the Boston shaker. Strain the contents of the shaker into the empty glass. Top the cocktail with lemon-lime soda. Garnish with a lime twist. Serve.

The last Viceroy of India was Louis Mountbatten, 1st Earl Mountbatten of Burma. He was an uncle to Prince Phillip and a second cousin once removed to Queen Elizabeth. Louis was the youngest son of Prince Louis of Battenberg. The prince and his family surrendered their princely titles in 1917 as the German empire fell and changed their names from Battenberg to the English Mountbatten. The same year, the elder Mountbatten was named the Marquess of Milford Haven. Louis's elder brother later succeeded to that title. For his service to the British empire, Louis was named Earl Mountbatten of Burma. Louis was killed in an IRA bombing in 1979. A special clause was placed in the letters patent that allowed the title to pass through his daughters. His grandson, Norton Knatchbull, 3rd Earl Mountbatten, succeeded his mother in 2017. Louis was known as "Dickey" within the royal family.

DICKEY WALLBANGER

1 ounce tequila
1 ounce vodka
4 ounces orange juice

Add ice to an old-fashioned glass. Add tequila, vodka, and orange juice. Serve.

A castle was a good way to stay safe from your enemy. The battering ram was a way to force entry into the castle through the weak spot, the front gate. Many castles were breached by this weapon of war.

ATTERING RAM

1 ounce tequila
1 ounce vodka
4 ounces energy drink

Add ice to an old-fashioned glass. Pour the tequila, vodka, and energy drink into the glass. Serve.

On the border of Spain and France sits the landlocked principality of Andorra. According to a charter of 1278, the government of Andorra is headed by co-princes, the Bishop of Urgell and the head of state of France (president of France). If you are born a commoner, one way to become a prince is to be elected the president of France.

ORDER CROSSING

1½ ounces tequila
5 ounces cola
¼ ounce lime juice

¼ ounce lemon juice
Lime wedge

Add ice to a highball glass. Add the lemon juice, lime juice, and tequila. Stir. Fill with the glass with cola. Garnish with lime wedge. Serve.

The story of Don Quixote is about a hidalgo (noble) who has lost touch with reality and goes on a quest to bring back chivalry.

ON QUIXOTE

¾ ounce tequila
¾ ounce Guinness Stout

Prepare a shot glass. Add the tequila and then the Guinness to the shot glass. Serve.

St. George is the patron saint of England, Ethiopia, Georgia, and the Catalonia region of Spain. The warrior St. George is known for slaying the dragon and saving a princess. St. George's Day is celebrated each year on April 23.

RAGON SLAYER

¾ ounce tequila
¾ ounce Green Chartreuse

Prepare a shot glass. Add the tequila and then the Green Chartreuse to the shot glass. Serve.

The sun never sets on the British empire or British Commonwealth. Every night leads to a sunrise. If a monarch is going to start the morning with a drink, consider the Tequila Sunrise.

TEQUILA SUNRISE

1½ ounces tequila
3 ounces orange juice
½ ounce grenadine syrup
Orange slice
Cocktail cherry

Add ice to an old-fashioned glass to chill the glass. Add tequila and orange juice. Add the grenadine, which will sink to the bottom of the glass, then stir gently. Garnish with orange slice and cocktail cherry. Serve.

BRANDY COCKTAILS

Brandy is distilled wine. Most brandy has a golden hue from barrel aging; however, some brandy is clear because the barrels were old, used barrels with no color left to lend to the brandy or the brandy was not aged at all. Cognac, Armagnac, and Calvados are three examples of famous French brandy. Cognac is distilled from a wine made from a mixture of mostly ugni blanc (Trebbiano), Folle blanche, and Colombard grapes, with small amounts of other varietals permitted. Cognac comes from the Cognac region just north of Bordeaux. Armagnac starts as grape wine from ten different grapes, but mostly these are the same grapes used to make cognac. Armagnac is produced in the Armagnac region in Gascony in southwest France. Calvados begins as apple wine in the northern Normandy region of France.

The longer brandy is aged, the higher the price. For cocktails, you may consider using younger product unless you are trying to make a statement—but know that the subtle differences that are clear to the palate are lost in the mixture of a cocktail. Brandy is made in the Americas and examples come from both North and South America. Cognac, Armagnac, and Calvados are all considered luxury products, which is why they would be the product of choice of a royal with a seemingly unlimited expense account.

Sophie, Duchess of Hohenberg, did not share her husband's title. As the daughter of a count, Sophie was not considered marrying material for Archduke Franz Ferdinand of Austria, who was the heir to the imperial throne. The archduke had to swear that Sophie would not become empress and their children would not be heirs to the throne because they would be a product of a morganatic marriage. Most of the imperial family boycotted their wedding.

ARCHDUCHESS

1½ ounces brandy
½ ounce raspberry liqueur
1 scoop vanilla ice cream
1 raspberry

To a blender, add the vanilla ice cream, brandy, and raspberry liqueur. Blend until smooth. Pour into a cocktail glass. Garnish with a raspberry. Serve.

The city of Baltimore, Maryland, borrows the name of Cecil Calvert, 2nd Baron Baltimore. The state of Maryland borrows Lord Baltimore's coat of arms. Although Baltimore and

Maryland both live on, the Barons Baltimore ceased to exist in 1771, when Frederick Calvert, 6th Baron Baltimore, passed away at age forty without a legitimate heir.

BALTIMORE EGGNOG

1 ounce cognac
1 ounce dark rum
½ ounce Madeira
1 egg

½ ounce simple syrup
½ ounce half-and-half
½ ounce milk

Add ice and water to a Collins glass to chill the glass. Add ice to the tin side of a Boston shaker. In the mixing glass, add cognac, dark rum, Madeira, egg, simple syrup, half-and-half, and milk. Pour the contents of the mixing glass into the iced tin and secure the glass to the tin. Shake the contents until the ice sounds different and the contents are cold. Open the Boston shaker. Empty the Collins glass, then strain the contents of the shaker into the empty glass. Serve.

Catherine de' Medici was the queen consort for Henry II. The two had many children together, five of whom would become a king or a queen consort. Catherine witnessed three sons take the throne of France: Francis II, Charles IX, and Henry III. Her daughter Elisabeth was the queen consort of Spain, and her daughter Margaret was the queen consort of France to Henry IV.

ℬOUQUET DE PARIS

2 ounces cognac
1 ounce apricot brandy
¼ ounce grenadine
¼ ounce lemon juice
Lemon twist

Add ice to an old-fashioned glass. Add ice to the tin side of a Boston shaker. In the mixing glass, add cognac, apricot brandy, grenadine, and lemon juice. Pour the contents of the mixing glass into the iced tin and secure the glass to the tin. Shake the contents until the ice sounds different and the contents are cold. Open the Boston shaker. Strain the contents of the shaker into the empty glass. Garnish with lemon twist. Serve.

The Three Emperors Dinner (Dîner des Trois Empereurs) was a meal fit for . . . well, three emperors. The meal included sixteen courses and eight wines served over an eight-hour meal at the Café Anglais in Paris. Attending was Tsar Alexander II; his son, who would become Tsar Alexander III; and the host, King William of Prussia (who would become the German emperor). Also attending was Prince Otto von Bismarck.

AFÉ ROYALE

1 sugar cube
1 ounce cognac
1 ounce coffee liqueur
4 ounces coffee

Soak the sugar cube in the cognac. Add the coffee liqueur to a coffee cup and fill with coffee. Flame the cognac-soaked sugar cube until the flame burns out, then add the remains to the coffee. Serve.

Louis XIV, known as the Sun King, is the longest-serving monarch in European history with a reign of almost seventy-two and a third years. Louis ascended the French throne at age four. He outlived his eldest son, Louis, Grand Dauphin, and his grandson, Louis, Duke of Burgundy and Dauphin, so when Louis died at the age of seventy-six, his great-grandson succeeded the throne as Louis XV.

CORONATION COCKTAIL #4

2 ounces cognac
¼ ounce Cointreau
1 dash orange bitters
Sprig of mint
Small mint leaves
Lemon twist

Add ice and water to a cocktail glass to chill the glass. Add ice to the tin side of a Boston shaker. In the mixing glass, add cognac, Cointreau, orange bitters, and mint sprig. Pour the contents of the mixing glass into the iced tin and secure the glass to the tin. Shake the contents until the ice sounds different and the contents are cold. Open the Boston shaker. Empty the cocktail glass, then strain the contents of the shaker into the empty glass. Garnish with a small mint leaf and a lemon twist. Serve.

Henry III of France was king of two countries and grand duke of another. Usually when a prince has two older brothers, there is little chance that the prince will become king. This was the case for Henry III. In 1573, when he was offered the Kingdom of Poland and Grand Duchy of Lithuania, he took the opportunity. When his brother Charles IX died in 1574, Henry was able to take the French throne, so he abandoned Poland and Lithuania.

HENRY III COFFEE

1 ounce cognac
1 ounce coffee liqueur
1 ounce Mandarine Napoléon
3 ounces coffee

Warm the coffee cup with hot water. Once the cup is warm, discard the water. Add the cognac, coffee liqueur, and Mandarine Napoléon, then top with coffee. Serve.

King Charles II granted Connecticut a royal charter, recognizing the colony in 1662. In 1675, Sir Edmund Andros, the newly appointed governor of New York, claimed that Connecticut fell under his control and demanded that the colonists surrender the charter. Instead of yielding the charter, legend claims the colonists hid it in a very large white oak tree. The Glorious Revolution would solve the "Andros issue." A storm destroyed the tree in 1856. The wood was salvaged and carved into furniture that is featured at the capitol building in Hartford, Connecticut. The oak tree has been commemorated several times. In 1935, it was placed on stamps and a half dollar. The Charter Oak was also featured on one of the 1999 quarters. Old Charter Bourbon features the name of the famous oak tree, which Charter Oak State College does as well.

AK TREE

1 ounce Armagnac (or bourbon)
1 ounce amaretto
1 ounce coffee liqueur
3 ounces milk

Add ice to a Collins glass. Add ice to the tin side of a Boston shaker. In the mixing glass, add brandy, amaretto, coffee liqueur, and milk. Pour the contents of the mixing glass into the iced tin and secure the glass to the tin. Shake the contents until the ice sounds different and the contents are cold. Open the Boston shaker. Strain the contents of the shaker into the ice-filled glass. Serve.

Few princes can negotiate their title when their wives become queen. However, the Dutch Prince of Orange, William, did just that when his wife, Mary, was offered the throne in 1689, following the Glorious Revolution. Mary was already tapped to become queen and William the prince consort, but William negotiated a joint monarchy that included his ability to continue to rule in the case that Mary predeceased him. He lived eight years beyond Mary. They ruled as William III and II and Mary II.

ILLEM VAN ORANJE

2 ounces cognac
1 ounce Cointreau
3 dashes orange bitters
Orange twist

Add ice and water to a cocktail glass to chill the glass. Add ice to the tin side of a Boston shaker. In the mixing glass, add cognac, Cointreau, and orange bitters. Pour the contents of the mixing glass into the iced tin and secure the glass to the tin. Shake the contents until the ice sounds different and the contents are cold. Open the Boston shaker. Empty the cocktail glass, then strain the contents of the shaker into the empty glass. Garnish with an orange twist. Serve.

The 2004 film *The Prince and Me* starring Julia Stiles was a fictional story about Denmark's crown prince traveling incognito to the United States and meeting his future bride. In 1999, Máxima, a young lady from Argentina who was traveling in Spain, met a man who introduced himself simply as

Alexander. The relationship progressed, and Alexander had to admit he had not been completely truthful when they met . . . really, he was Willem-Alexander, the Prince of Orange, and the heir apparent to the throne of the Kingdom of the Netherlands. At first, Máxima thought the prince was joking. The relationship continued, and the couple married. In 2013, the prince ascended the Dutch throne as king of the Netherlands, Máxima at his side as the queen consort. The royal couple now have three daughters.

*I*NTERNATIONAL COCKTAIL

1½ ounces cognac
1 ounce triple sec
1 ounce anisette
½ ounce vodka

Add ice and water to a cocktail glass to chill the glass. Add ice to the tin side of a Boston shaker. In the mixing glass, add cognac, triple sec, anisette, and vodka. Pour the contents of the mixing glass into the iced tin and secure the glass to the tin. Shake the contents until the ice sounds different and the contents are cold. Open the Boston shaker. Empty the cocktail glass, then strain the contents of the shaker into the empty glass. Serve.

A prince is very likely to become a royal knight fairly young. This tradition dates back to when royal and noble men were expected to fight in the field either to defend the country or to expand the domain.

IR KNIGHT

2 ounces cognac
½ ounce Cointreau
½ ounce Green Chartreuse
1 dash Angostura bitters
Lemon twist

Add ice and water to a cocktail glass to chill the glass. Add ice to the tin side of a Boston shaker. In the mixing glass, add cognac, Cointreau, Green Chartreuse, and Angostura bitters. Pour the contents of the mixing glass into the iced tin and secure the glass to the tin. Shake the contents until the ice sounds different and the contents are cold. Open the Boston shaker. Empty the cocktail glass, then strain the contents of the shaker into the empty glass. Garnish with a lemon twist. Serve.

When a small privileged class rules, an aristocracy exists.

RISTOCRACY

1 ounce apricot brandy
1 ounce crème de banana
½ ounce white crème de cacao
½ ounce coconut cream

Add ice and water to a cocktail glass to chill the glass. Add ice to the tin side of a Boston shaker. In the mixing glass, add apricot brandy, crème de banana, white crème de cacao, and coconut cream. Pour the contents of the mixing glass into the iced tin and secure the glass to the tin. Shake the contents until the ice sounds different and the contents are cold. Open the Boston shaker. Empty the cocktail glass, then strain the contents of the shaker into the empty glass. Serve.

Douglas Fairbanks Jr. was an American actor and World War II hero who was awarded a Silver Star. Fairbanks was already an established actor who had played many "English" roles, such as Robin Hood, when World War II erupted. He received decorations from France, Great Britain, Brazil, Italy, and West Germany. Later, he was granted an honorary knighthood by the British.

AIRBANKS

¾ ounce apricot brandy
¾ ounce gin
¾ ounce dry vermouth
¼ ounce grenadine
¼ ounce lemon juice
Lemon twist

Add ice and water to a cocktail glass to chill the glass. Add ice to the tin side of a Boston shaker. In the mixing glass, add apricot brandy, gin, dry vermouth, grenadine, and lemon juice. Pour the contents of the mixing glass into the iced tin and secure the glass to the tin. Shake the contents until the ice sounds different and the contents are cold. Open the Boston shaker. Empty the cocktail glass, then strain the

contents of the shaker into the empty glass. Garnish with a
lemon twist. Serve.

According to David Embury, the Jack Rose is one of the six cocktails that, similar to the sidecar, everyone should know how to make. The name invokes the British crown because of the Union Jack and the English rose.

ACK ROSE

2 ounces apple brandy
½ ounce fresh lemon juice
¼ ounce grenadine
Superfine sugar

Set up the cocktail glasses ahead of time. Dip the edge of the cocktail glass in water, then dip in a plate of superfine sugar for a thin, even frost on the edge of the glass. Then freeze the glass. Add ice to the tin side of a Boston shaker. In the mixing glass, add the apple brandy, lemon juice, and grenadine. Pour the contents of the mixing glass into the iced tin and secure the glass to the tin. Shake the contents until the ice sounds different and the contents are cold. Open the Boston shaker. Strain the contents of the shaker into the empty glass. Serve.

In 1811, George IV, still Prince of Wales, took the role of prince regent while his father, George III, suffered from porphyria. The prince regent would become king in 1820.

PRINCE REGENT

1 ounce apricot brandy
1 ounce white crème de cacao
1 ounce chocolate milk

Add ice and water to a cocktail glass to chill the glass. Add ice to the tin side of a Boston shaker. In the mixing glass, add the apricot brandy, white crème de cacao, and chocolate milk. Pour the contents of the mixing glass into the iced tin and secure the glass to the tin. Shake the contents until the ice sounds different and the contents are cold. Open the Boston shaker. Empty the cocktail glass, then strain the contents of the shaker into the empty glass. Serve.

Everyone loves a good royal wedding. In 2018, Prince Harry and Meghan, Duke and Duchess of Sussex, enjoyed an international celebration that brought royals, Hollywood stars, and the world together.

ROYAL WEDDING

1 ounce apricot brandy
1 ounce Cointreau
½ ounce lime juice
Lime wheel

Add ice and water to a cocktail glass to chill the glass. Add ice to the tin side of a Boston shaker. In the mixing glass, add apricot brandy, Cointreau, and lime juice. Pour the contents

*of the mixing glass into the iced tin and secure the glass to
the tin. Shake the contents until the ice sounds different and
the contents are cold. Open the Boston shaker. Empty the
cocktail glass, then strain the contents of the shaker into the
empty glass. Garnish with a lime wheel. Serve.*

Prince Harry, Duke of Sussex, served two deployments in
Afghanistan, during which time the Taliban targeted the
prince to be kidnapped or killed. He served as copilot of an
Apache helicopter.

RAVE SOLDIER

1 ounce cherry brandy
½ ounce Southern Comfort
½ ounce passion fruit liqueur
½ ounce lemon juice
½ ounce sweet and sour mix
Lemon twist

*Add ice and water to a cocktail glass to chill the glass. Add
ice to the tin side of a Boston shaker. In the mixing glass,
add cherry brandy, Southern Comfort, passion fruit liqueur,
lemon juice, and sweet and sour mix. Pour the contents of the
mixing glass into the iced tin and secure the glass to the tin.
Shake the contents until the ice sounds different and the contents are cold. Open the Boston shaker. Empty the cocktail
glass, then strain the contents of the shaker into the empty
glass. Garnish with a lemon twist. Serve.*

Many kings and emperors took concubines both in Europe and in Asia. In many cases, the children from these relationships were not eligible to inherit title, land, or property.

$\mathscr{C}$ONCUBINE

1 ounce cherry brandy
1 ounce amaretto
1 ounce cream

Add ice and water to a cocktail glass to chill the glass. Add ice to the tin side of a Boston shaker. In the mixing glass, add cherry brandy, amaretto, and cream. Pour the contents of the mixing glass into the iced tin and secure the glass to the tin. Shake the contents until the ice sounds different and the contents are cold. Open the Boston shaker. Empty the cocktail glass, then strain the contents of the shaker into the empty glass. Serve.

Prince Arthur, Duke of Connaught and Strathearn, was the third son of Queen Victoria and Prince Albert. He served as the governor-general of Canada from 1911 to 1916. He lived until 1942 and died at the age of ninety-one.

$\mathscr{G}$ENERAL

1½ ounces cherry brandy
1 ounce cranberry juice cocktail
½ ounce grenadine
1 ounce club soda

Add ice to an old-fashioned glass. Add the cherry brandy, cranberry juice, grenadine, and club soda. Stir. Serve.

Prince Henry the Navigator was a sponsor of Portuguese exploration in the early fifteenth century. His father was King John I of Portugal; therefore he was related to the Portuguese and Spanish crowns on his father's side. His mother was Philippa of Lancaster, the sister of King Henry IV of England; therefore he was related to the English and French crowns on his mother's side.

ERCHANT PRINCE

1 ounce cherry brandy
¾ ounce vodka
¾ ounce Drambuie
¾ ounce vanilla liqueur

Add ice and water to a cocktail glass to chill the glass. Add ice to the tin side of a Boston shaker. In the mixing glass, add cherry brandy, vodka, Drambuie, and vanilla liqueur. Pour the contents of the mixing glass into the iced tin and secure the glass to the tin. Shake the contents until the ice sounds different and the contents are cold. Open the Boston shaker. Empty the cocktail glass, then strain the contents of the shaker into the empty glass. Serve.

For more than a thousand years, the city of Venice elected one of the elders of the city. The election was for life, during which time the Doge of Venice was confined to the Doge's

Palace and St. Mark's Basilica. The last Doge of Venice was Ludovico Manin, who was forced to abdicate in 1797 by Napoleon Bonaparte.

ENICE

1 ounce Scotch
1 ounce cherry brandy
1 ounce sherry

Add ice and water to a cocktail glass to chill the glass. Add ice to the tin side of a Boston shaker. In the mixing glass, add Scotch, cherry brandy, and sherry. Pour the contents of the mixing glass into the iced tin and secure the glass to the tin. Shake the contents until the ice sounds different and the contents are cold. Open the Boston shaker. Empty the cocktail glass, then strain the contents of the shaker into the empty glass. Serve.

Uther Pendragon was the legendary father of King Arthur. According to legend, the ruins of Pendragon's castle are located in Cumbria, England. The castle is known as Pendragon Castle.

ENDRAGON

1½ ounces Armagnac
1 ounce cream
⅔ ounce blackberry liqueur
½ ounce kirschwasser

Add ice and water to a cocktail glass to chill the glass. Add ice to the tin side of a Boston shaker. In the mixing glass, add Armagnac, cream, blackberry liqueur, and kirschwasser. Pour the contents of the mixing glass into the iced tin and secure the glass to the tin. Shake the contents until the ice sounds different and the contents are cold. Open the Boston shaker. Empty the cocktail glass, then strain the contents of the shaker into the empty glass. Serve.

The Glorious Revolution of 1688 established two lines of succession to the British throne, the legitimate line and the Jacobite line. Jacobite Charles Edward Stuart, also known as Bonnie Prince Charlie, was the grandson of James II, who lived in continental Europe. The young prince invaded Scotland in 1745 but had limited success in really retaking the throne. He returned to Europe and lived out the rest of his life.

ONNIE PRINCE CHARLIE

1½ ounces cognac
¾ ounce Drambuie
¾ ounce lime juice

Add ice and water to a cocktail glass to chill the glass. Add ice to the tin side of a Boston shaker. In the mixing glass, add cognac, Drambuie, and lime juice. Pour the contents of the mixing glass into the iced tin and secure the glass to the tin. Shake the contents until the ice sounds different and the contents are cold. Open the Boston shaker. Empty the cocktail glass, then strain the contents of the shaker into the empty glass. Serve.

When Henry III was crowned after the death of his father, King John, he had to reestablish royal authority. He is one of a few monarchs that enjoyed two coronations. The first was in 1216, nine days after the death of his father, at Gloucester Cathedral. The second coronation was in 1220 at Westminster Abbey. A long reign of fifty-six years allowed him to repair much of the damage his father had caused. He ruled England until 1272.

CORONATION COCKTAIL #3

1 ounce applejack or Calvados
1 ounce dry vermouth
1 ounce sweet vermouth
¼ ounce apricot liqueur
Lemon twist

Add ice and water to a cocktail glass to chill the glass. Add ice to the mixing glass, then add applejack, dry vermouth, sweet vermouth, and apricot liqueur. Stir at least forty times. Strain the contents of the shaker into the empty glass. Garnish with a lemon twist. Serve.

WHISKEY COCKTAILS

Whiskey (whisky) is the largest differentiated spirit category. This spirit is traditionally made in Scotland, Ireland, Canada, and the United States. Whiskey is distilled from beer made from grain. Each tradition uses a different grain or a grain mixture for the distiller's beer. The beer is then distilled into a clear spirit and aged in oak barrels for a short or extended period. The longer the whiskey is aged, the higher the price of the spirit.

Most Scotch whisky is made from malt and grain whiskies and is aged in a variety of used barrels, including bourbon, sherry, and port barrels. Scotch has a unique smoked peaty flavor and aroma. Most Scotch is aged for at least four years but can be aged for much, much longer. Irish whiskey has a light and mild flavor and aroma and can be made from a variety of grains. This spirit is aged for at least three years but many Irish whiskies are aged longer. Canadian whisky is mild flavored, made from multiple grains, and aged for at least three years. Bourbon is one of the most highly regulated whiskies made in the United States (95% is made in Kentucky). It is made from at least 51 percent corn (most bourbon distillers use more—closer to 65–75%). As bourbon comes off the still, it must be less than 160 proof. Only water can be added to bourbon. As bourbon is added to newly charred oak barrels, the proof can't exceed 125 proof and can't be less than 80 proof. There is no minimum age for bourbon, but if the bourbon is aged less than two years, there must be an age statement on the label. Most bourbon is aged for at least four years. Other whiskies are usually defined by the grain from which they are primary made. For example, corn whiskey is at least 80 percent corn, rye whiskey is at least 51 percent rye, and wheat whiskey is at least 51 percent wheat.

David, as he was known to the royal family, will always be known as the man who gave up a kingdom for the woman he loved. His full name was Edward Albert Christian George Andrew Patrick David Windsor. He was born in 1894 and named to be king. The names George, Andrew, Patrick, and David are the patron saints of the four corners of Great Britain. At the moment his father, George V, died in 1936, David ascended the throne as King Edward VIII. But even as king, he was not allowed to marry the twice-divorced Wallis Simpson. So he quit and formally abdicated, never having been crowned. His brother would ascend as George VI, and Edward was created the Duke of Windsor. The former king married Simpson. He would live away from Great Britain for the rest of his life, visiting occasionally.

$\mathcal{E}$DWARD VIII COCKTAIL

1½ ounces Canadian whisky
1 dash absinthe
¼ ounce sweet vermouth
¼ ounce water
Orange twist

Fill an old-fashioned glass with ice. Add the Canadian whisky, absinthe, sweet vermouth, and water, and stir. Garnish with an orange twist. Serve.

Every year the city of New Orleans crowns a new king (Rex). The Big Easy is named for Philippe II, Duke of Orleans, who served as the regent for the Kingdom of France from 1715 until 1723. Arnaud's restaurant is located in the French Quarter. The restaurant was founded in 1918 by Arnaud Cazenave, who styled himself a "count."

$\mathcal{A}$RNAUD'S SPECIAL

1 dash Peychaud's Bitters
1 dash Angostura bitters
2 ounces bourbon

2 dashes absinthe
Lemon twist

Add ice to an old-fashioned glass. Add the bitters, bourbon, and absinthe, and then stir. Add more ice if needed. Stir again. Twist the lemon twist over the top of the glass and rub against the rim of the glass. Add the twist to the drink. Serve.

Prince Albert, Queen Victoria's consort, purchased the Scottish Balmoral Castle in 1852 for the royal family's use. The huge estate is still owned by the royal family.

ALMORAL

1½ ounces Scotch
½ ounce sweet vermouth
½ ounce dry vermouth
2 dashes Angostura bitters

Add ice and water to a cocktail glass to chill the glass. Add ice to the tin side of a Boston shaker. In the mixing glass, add Scotch, sweet vermouth, dry vermouth, and Angostura bitters. Pour the contents of the mixing glass into the iced tin and secure the glass to the tin. Shake the contents until the ice sounds different and the contents are cold. Open the Boston shaker. Empty the cocktail glass, then strain the contents of the shaker into the empty glass. Serve.

Sir William Wallace was a Scottish knight who led a revolt against the English occupation of Scotland during the reign of Edward I of England, "Edward Longshanks," in a period of interregnum in Scotland. Wallace would rise to the rank and responsibilities of Guardian of the Kingdom of Scotland. Wallace was captured and given to Edward, who had Wallace hanged, emasculated, eviscerated, drawn, quartered, and beheaded for treason. Wallace asked how his actions were treasonous, as he, as a Scotsman, was never a subject of the King of England. Wallace was immortalized in the Academy Award–winning film *Braveheart*, starring and directed by Mel Gibson.

BRAVEHEART

2 ounces Scotch whisky
1 ounce lemon juice
½ ounce honey simple syrup
½ teaspoon fresh ginger juice
3 dashes Angostura bitters

Add ice to an old-fashioned glass. Add ice to the tin side of a Boston shaker. In the mixing glass, add Scotch whisky, lemon juice, honey simple syrup, fresh ginger juice, and Angostura bitters. Pour the contents of the mixing glass into the iced tin and secure the glass to the tin. Shake the contents until the ice sounds different and the contents are cold. Open the Boston shaker. Strain the contents of the shaker into the ice-filled old-fashioned glass. Serve.

In 1725, King George I authorized the formation of the Black Watch to help control the Highlands in Scotland. The unit is now known as Black Watch, 3rd Battalion, Royal Regiment of Scotland. The blue, green, and black weave in its tartan makes the Black Watch easy to recognize.

LACK WATCH

1½ ounces Scotch
1½ ounces coffee liqueur
1 ounce club soda

Add ice to an old-fashioned glass. Add the Scotch, coffee liqueur, and club soda. Stir and serve.

A Scottish clan is a recognized family group based on family relationship. A clan is recognized by its tartan. A member of the clan is known as a clansman.

LANSMAN'S COFFEE

2 ounces Scotch
4 ounces hot coffee

Add the Scotch and coffee to a coffee cup. Serve.

Most Scottish clans have a chief to lead the clan. Historically, the clan chief led the clan in battle.

LAN CHIEFTAIN

2 ounces Scotch
1 ounce Cointreau
Splash orange juice
Orange twist

Add ice and water to a cocktail glass to chill the glass. Add ice to the tin side of a Boston shaker. In the mixing glass, add Scotch, Cointreau, and orange juice. Pour the contents of the mixing glass into the iced tin and secure the glass to the tin. Shake the contents until the ice sounds different and the contents are cold. Open the Boston shaker. Empty the cocktail glass, then strain the contents of the shaker into the empty glass. Garnish with an orange twist. Serve.

Eleanor of Aquitaine is an incredible historical figure. She was the Duchess of the Aquitaine in her own right from 1137 to 1204, and she took part in battles, including some in the Second Crusade. The Aquitaine was rich in resources and ports. He who married the duchess could control the ports and the riches; the Aquitaine was an important French province and would be a welcome acquisition. She married King Louis VII of France in 1137, but soon she petitioned the pope for an annulment. In 1152, an annulment was granted on the grounds of consanguinity (the idea that the two were closely related by blood); in reality, no son and heir had been produced in fifteen years of marriage. Eleanor would marry the Duke of Normandy in 1152, who would become Henry II of England in 1154. They produced eight children, including three kings and two queen consorts: Henry the Young King,

Richard the Lionhearted, John, Eleanor of Castile, and Joan of Sicily.

$\mathscr{F}$RENCH ACQUISITION

1 ounce Scotch
1 ounce sweet vermouth
1 ounce dry vermouth
Splash of Cointreau
Orange twist

Add ice and water to a cocktail glass to chill the glass. Add ice to the tin side of a Boston shaker. In the mixing glass, add Scotch, sweet vermouth, dry vermouth, and Cointreau. Pour the contents of the mixing glass into the iced tin and secure the glass to the tin. Shake the contents until the ice sounds different and the contents are cold. Open the Boston shaker. Empty the cocktail glass, then strain the contents of the shaker into the empty glass. Garnish with the orange twist. Serve.

The monarch is usually the grand master of knightly orders. However, the sovereign may appoint someone the title of grand master for an order in their place.

GRAND MASTER

2 ounces Scotch
½ ounce peppermint schnapps
4 ounces club soda
Lemon twist

Add ice to a highball glass. Add the Scotch, peppermint schnapps, and club soda. Garnish with the lemon twist. Serve.

Macbeth was the King of Alba (part of Scotland) from 1040 to 1057. Although a real king, Macbeth will forever be remembered as protagonist of the William Shakespeare tragedy *Macbeth*. In the play, Macbeth stabs King Duncan and then claims the throne of Scotland. In the end, Macduff kills Macbeth in battle and Duncan's son, Malcolm, prepares to be crowned.

MACBETH

2 ounces Scotch
¼ ounce blue curaçao
¼ ounce amaretto
½ ounce lemon juice
Splash of simple syrup

Add ice and water to a cocktail glass to chill the glass. Add ice to the tin side of a Boston shaker. In the mixing glass, add Scotch, blue curaçao, amaretto, lemon juice, and simple syrup. Pour the contents of the mixing glass into the iced tin and secure the glass to the tin. Shake the contents until the ice sounds different and the contents are cold. Open the Boston shaker. Empty the cocktail glass, then strain the contents of the shaker into the empty glass. Serve.

Lord Macduff was the hero in the play *Macbeth*. The title currently belongs to David Carnegie, 4th Duke of Fife, who is also the 13th Earl of Southesk and the 4th Earl of Macduff. The duke was styled Earl of Macduff (Lord Macduff), by courtesy, from his birth in 1961 until 1992, when he was styled the Earl of Southesk, by courtesy, from 1992 to 2015. In 2015 he succeeded as the Duke of Fife and truly became the Earl of Macduff.

ACDUFF

2 ounces Scotch
¾ ounce Cointreau
2 dashes Angostura bitters
Orange twist

Add ice and water to a cocktail glass to chill the glass. Add ice to the tin side of a Boston shaker. In the mixing glass, add Scotch, Cointreau, and bitters. Pour the contents of the mixing glass into the iced tin and secure the glass to the tin. Shake the contents until the ice sounds different and the contents are cold. Open the Boston shaker. Empty the cocktail glass, then strain the contents of the shaker into the empty glass. Garnish with an orange twist. Serve.

James II and VII was the last Roman Catholic monarch of England, Ireland, and Scotland. During the Glorious Revolution of 1688, he was replaced by co-monarchs—his daughter, Mary II, and her husband, William III and II.

JAMES THE SECOND COMES FIRST

2 ounces Scotch
½ ounce tawny port
½ ounce dry vermouth
Dash Angostura bitters

Add ice and water to a cocktail glass to chill the glass. Add ice to the tin side of a Boston shaker. In the mixing glass, add Scotch, tawny port, dry vermouth, and Angostura bitters. Pour the contents of the mixing glass into the iced tin and secure the glass to the tin. Shake the contents until the ice sounds different and the contents are cold. Open the Boston shaker. Empty the cocktail glass, then strain the contents of the shaker into the empty glass. Serve.

Prince Edward of Woodstock was known as the Black Prince, likely for the black armor he wore in battle. He was created the Duke of Cornwall in 1337, the Prince of Wales in 1343, and heir of King Edward III. He died in 1376, before his father. His surviving son, Richard, would become the heir to England and would inherit as King Richard II in 1377.

RINCE OF DARKNESS

1½ ounces Scotch
1 ounce coffee liqueur
½ ounce club soda

Add ice to an old-fashioned glass. Add the Scotch, coffee liqueur, and club soda, and then stir. Serve.

Mary Queen of Scots was both the queen of Scotland (1542–1567) and the queen consort of France (1559–1560). She claimed to be the queen of England too. Her cousin, Elizabeth, the last Tudor queen of England, eventually captured and beheaded Mary. Mary's son, James VI of Scotland (1567–1625), would become James I of England (1603–1625).

QUEEN OF SCOTS

2 ounces Scotch
¼ ounce Chartreuse
¼ ounce blue curaçao
¼ ounce simple syrup
¼ ounce lemon juice
Lemon twist

Add ice and water to a cocktail glass to chill the glass. Add ice to the tin side of a Boston shaker. In the mixing glass, add Scotch, Chartreuse, blue curaçao, simple syrup, and lemon juice. Pour the contents of the mixing glass into the iced tin and secure the glass to the tin. Shake the contents until the ice sounds different and the contents are cold. Open the Boston shaker. Empty the cocktail glass, then strain the contents of the shaker into the empty glass. Garnish with a lemon twist. Serve.

Robert Roy MacGregor, "Rob Roy," (1671–1734) was a Scottish outlaw who is now a hero. Lady Randolph Churchill (Jennie Jerome) was an American who became part of an English noble family and mother to a prime minister, Winston Churchill. Both have connections to similar drinks created on the Island of Manhattan in New York. A Rob Roy is a simple cocktail named for the hero, while the lore of Manhattan connects Jennie Jerome with the cocktail. What we know is true—both cocktails were created in Manhattan.

OB ROY AND THE MANHATTAN

2 ounces Scotch (Rob Roy) or bourbon (Manhattan)
1 ounce sweet vermouth
2 dashes Angostura bitters
Cocktail cherry

For a Rob Roy add ice and water to a cocktail glass to chill the glass. In the mixing glass, add ice, Scotch, sweet vermouth, and Angostura bitters. Stir thirty to forty times. Empty the cocktail glass, then strain the contents of the mixing glass into the empty glass. Garnish with cocktail cherry. Serve.
For a Manhattan, substitute bourbon for the Scotch.

Ireland claimed three hereditary knighthoods dating back to the fourteenth century: the White Knight, the Black Knight, and the Green Knight. The Fitzgibbon family was granted the title White Knight. Maurice Fitzgibbon was the 1st White Knight. The knighthood became dormant in 1611. The last Black Knight, Desmond FitzGerald, 29th Knight of Glin, passed away in 2011. The current Green Knight is Sir Adrian FitzGerald, 5th Baronet of Valentia, 23rd Knight of Kerry.

WHITE KNIGHT

1 ounce Scotch
1 ounce coffee liqueur
1 ounce cream

Add ice and water to a cocktail glass to chill the glass. Add ice to the tin side of a Boston shaker. In the mixing glass, add Scotch, coffee liqueur, and cream. Pour the contents of the mixing glass into the iced tin and secure the glass to the tin. Shake the contents until the ice sounds different and the contents are cold. Open the Boston shaker. Empty the cocktail glass, then strain the contents of the shaker into the empty glass. Serve.

The Royal Navy has the rank of commodore, which is equivalent to a United States rear admiral (lower half).

COMMODORE

1½ ounces bourbon
1 ounce crème de cacao
1 ounce lemon juice
Dash grenadine

Add ice and water to a cocktail glass to chill the glass. Add ice to the tin side of a Boston shaker. In the mixing glass, add bourbon, crème de cacao, lemon juice, and grenadine. Pour the contents of the mixing glass into the iced tin and secure the glass to the tin. Shake the contents until the ice sounds different and the contents are cold. Open the Boston shaker. Empty the cocktail glass, then strain the contents of the shaker into the empty glass. Serve.

A crowned head is any monarch. The term *crowned heads* is used to describe all of the monarchs as a whole.

CROWNED HEAD

1½ ounces bourbon
1 ounce dry vermouth
¾ ounce blackberry liqueur
Splash lemon juice

Add ice and water to a cocktail glass to chill the glass. Add ice to the tin side of a Boston shaker. In the mixing glass, add bourbon, dry vermouth, blackberry liqueur, and lemon juice. Pour the contents of the mixing glass into the iced tin and secure the glass to the tin. Shake the contents until the ice sounds different and the contents are cold. Open the Boston shaker. Empty the cocktail glass, then strain the contents of the shaker into the empty glass. Serve.

Clan Hunter of Scotland is required to pay the sovereign a silver penny on the Feast of Pentecost when the sovereign visits. To this day, the clan keeps silver pennies in case the sovereign visits.

UNTER

1½ ounces bourbon
1 ounce cherry brandy
Cocktail cherry

Add ice and water to a cocktail glass to chill the glass. Add ice to the tin side of a Boston shaker. In the mixing glass, add bourbon and cherry brandy. Pour the contents of the mixing glass into the iced tin and secure the glass to the tin. Shake the contents until the ice sounds different and the contents are cold. Open the Boston shaker. Empty the cocktail glass, then strain the contents of the shaker into the empty glass. Garnish with a cocktail cherry. Serve.

Gilbert du Motier, Marquis de Lafayette, descended from a French noble family. Fortune smiled on Lafayette. With six years' experience as a commissioned officer, he was commissioned a major general at age nineteen, in 1776. He would serve throughout the American Revolutionary War. Later, he would return to France. During the French Revolution, he was imprisoned but was released by Napoleon in 1797. Finally, he helped with the restoration of the French monarchy but later opposed the autocratic rule.

LAFAYETTE

2 ounces bourbon
½ ounce dry vermouth
1 ounce egg white
¼ ounce simple syrup
Cocktail cherry

Add ice to an old-fashioned glass. Add ice to the tin side of a Boston shaker. In the mixing glass, add bourbon, dry vermouth, egg white, and simple syrup. Pour the contents of the mixing glass into the iced tin and secure the glass to the tin. Shake the contents until the ice sounds different and the contents are cold. Open the Boston shaker. Strain the contents of the shaker into the ice-filled glass. Garnish with a cocktail cherry. Serve.

Horse racing is known as the sport of kings and the king of sports. There is no better cocktail to consume while enjoying a day at the races than a mint julep.

INT JULEP

2 ounces bourbon whiskey
½ ounce simple syrup
10 fresh mint leaves
1 dash Angostura bitters
1 mint sprig

Add the simple syrup, Angostura bitters, and mint to a mint julep glass. Tap a muddler against the mint and the bottom of the glass to release the mint's oils. Add the bourbon to the glass, then top the glass with crushed ice. Clap the mint sprig between your hands. Garnish the glass with the mint sprig. Serve.

William Walford Astor was an American who immigrated to Great Britain and became a British subject in 1899. He was ennobled in 1916 as Baron Astor and in 1917 as Viscount Astor. His son Waldorf Astor would inherit his father's title, while younger brother John Jacob Astor would become Baron Astor of Hever. Both noble titles are still active today: William Waldorf Astor III is the 4th Viscount Astor, while his third cousin John Jacob Astor VIII is the 3rd Baron Astor of Hever.

ALDORF COCKTAIL

2 ounces rye whiskey
¾ ounce sweet vermouth
¼ ounce absinthe
2 dashes Angostura bitters

Add ice and water to a cocktail glass to chill the glass. Add ice to a mixing glass, then add rye, sweet vermouth, absinthe, and Angostura bitters. Empty the cocktail glass, then strain the contents of the shaker into the empty glass. Serve.

The Royal Mounted Canadian Police, known simply as the Mounties, is the Canadian national law enforcement agency tasked with counterintelligence. Canada is part of the British Commonwealth, and the Queen of Canada is Elizabeth II.

ROYAL MOUNTED POLICE

2 ounces Canadian whisky
½ ounce blue curaçao
½ ounce dry sherry
Orange twist

Add ice and water to a cocktail glass to chill the glass. Add ice to the tin side of a Boston shaker. In the mixing glass, add Canadian whisky, blue curaçao, and dry sherry. Pour the contents of the mixing glass into the iced tin and secure the glass to the tin. Shake the contents until the ice sounds different

*and the contents are cold. Open the Boston shaker. Empty
the cocktail glass, then strain the contents of the shaker into
the empty glass. Garnish with an orange twist. Serve.*

Old King Cole was a merry old soul . . . at least that is what the
nursery rhyme tells us. Perhaps it was because of this twist
on the old-fashioned.

OLD KING COLE

2 ounces bourbon
Sugar cube
2 dashes Angostura bitters
Orange slice
Pineapple slice

*Add the sugar cube, bitters, orange slice, and pineapple slice
to the bottom of an old-fashioned cocktail glass. Muddle
the sugar and the fruit. Add ice and the bourbon, then stir.
Serve.*

King Richard the Lionhearted is proof that even a hero king
can be held captive. In 1192, as Richard traveled back to Europe from the Middle East and the crusades, he was captured
by Leopold V, Duke of Austria, who eventually gave him to
Henry VI, the Holy Roman Emperor. Henry demanded one
hundred thousand pounds of silver for Richard's safe return.
In an act of treason, Richard's brother, John, with the help of
King Phillip of France, offered his own sum to keep Richard
imprisoned. Eventually, Richard was released.

ING'S RANSOM

¾ ounce bourbon whiskey
¾ ounce Goldschläger

Prepare a shot glass. Add ice to the tin side of a Boston shaker. In the mixing glass, add Goldschläger and bourbon whiskey. Pour the contents of the mixing glass into the iced tin and secure the glass to the tin. Shake the contents until the ice sounds different and the contents are cold. Open the Boston shaker. Strain the contents of the shaker into the empty shot glass. Serve.

King John ascended the English throne when his brother Richard died. By the time John died, he had lost most of the holdings in France he had inherited from his brother that his parents had accumulated. John was at war with his own barons, and he was on the run. As his party crossed a river, the king lost most of his luggage to the water, including the crown jewels, which were never recovered.

ℋING'S CROWN

2 ounces Canadian whisky
1 ounce lime juice
4 ounces lemon-lime soda
Lime wedge

Add ice to a highball glass. Add the lime juice and the Canadian whisky and stir. Top the glass off with lemon-lime soda. Garnish with a lime twist or a lime wedge. Serve.

Rumors claim that the Blarney Stone at Blarney Castle is really a piece of the Stone of Scone given to the owner of the castle by none other than Robert the Bruce for support against King Edward II of England. The Stone of Scone is used for the coronation of Scottish monarchs and now for British monarchs.

LARNEY STONE COCKTAIL

2 ounces Irish whiskey
¼ ounce Cointreau
¼ ounce anisette
¼ ounce maraschino liqueur
Orange twist

Add ice and water to a cocktail glass to chill the glass. Add ice to the tin side of a Boston shaker. In the mixing glass, add Irish whiskey, Cointreau, anisette, and maraschino liqueur. Pour the contents of the mixing glass into the iced tin and secure the glass to the tin. Shake the contents until the ice sounds different and the contents are cold. Open the Boston shaker. Empty the cocktail glass, then strain the contents of the shaker into the empty glass. Garnish the cocktail with the orange twist. Serve.

OTHER COCKTAILS

Modern alcoholic concoctions are made from an endless combination of alcoholic beverages from many categories, including beer, wine, spirits, and liqueurs. Beer and wine are both fermented beverages. Beer is made by boiling grains to extract the sugars for fermenting to an average of 5 percent alcohol by volume. Wine is usually made from grapes. The grapes are pressed to extract the juice, which is then fermented. Wine varies in alcohol volume from 5 percent to 15 percent, with fortified wine being even higher. Fortified wine is wine with added brandy. Liqueurs are flavored, sweetened alcoholic beverages that are featured in many cocktails and serve as standalone after-dinner drinks also known as cordials. The alcohol by volume range for most liqueurs is from 17 percent (34 proof) to 30 percent (60 proof) but can be higher than 50 percent (100 proof).

American beauty Rachel Meghan Markle walked away from a successful acting career to marry her real-life knight, Prince Harry, who was created Duke of Sussex the morning of their wedding in 2018. As his consort, Meghan is the Duchess of Sussex. Her most recent acting role was as Rachel Zane on the show *Suits*. The couple have a son, Archie Mountbatten-Windsor.

AMERICAN BEAUTY

¾ ounce brandy
¾ ounce dry vermouth
¾ ounce orange juice
½ ounce ruby port

¼ ounce grenadine
Dash white crème de menthe
Rose petals

Add ice and water to a cocktail glass to chill the glass. Add ice to the tin side of a Boston shaker. In the mixing glass, add brandy, dry vermouth, orange juice, grenadine, and white crème de menthe. Pour the contents of the mixing glass into the iced tin and secure the glass to the tin. Shake the contents until the ice sounds different and the contents are cold. Open the Boston shaker. Empty the cocktail glass, then strain the contents of the shaker into the empty glass. Float the ruby port on top and garnish with rose petals. Serve.

King George V was not born to be king. However, when his elder brother Prince Albert Victor, Duke of Clarence and Avondale, died during a flu pandemic in 1892 at the tender age of twenty-eight, George inherited not only his brother's place in line for the throne but also his brother's fiancée, Princess Mary of Teck. George was already a Royal Navy officer when his naval career was sidetracked for his royal vocation. He ascended the throne in 1910 when his father, Edward VII, died. He led the British empire through World War I, during which time he changed the family name from the German Saxe-Coburg-Gotha to the British-sounding Windsor. He was once quoted as saying, "My father was frightened of his mother [Queen Victoria]; I was frightened of my father, and I am dammed well going to see to it that my children are frightened of me." He also predicted the downfall of his eldest son, the future Edward VIII: "After I am dead, the boy will ruin himself in twelve months." Edward ruled less than twelve months (and was never crowned) before abdicating in favor of his younger brother, George VI.

ING GEORGE V

½ ounce gin
½ ounce Scotch
½ ounce white crème de cacao
½ ounce Cointreau
½ ounce lemon juice

Add ice and water to a cocktail glass to chill the glass. Add ice to the tin side of a Boston shaker. In the mixing glass, add gin, Scotch, white crème de cacao, Cointreau, and lemon juice. Pour the contents of the mixing glass into the iced tin and secure the glass to the tin. Shake the contents until the ice sounds different and the contents are cold. Open the Boston shaker. Empty the cocktail glass, then strain the contents of the shaker into the empty glass. Serve.

Charlemagne was crowned on Christmas Day in 800 by Pope Leo III. He was already both king of the Franks and king of the Lombards. His empire included most of modern-day France and Germany and part of modern-day Italy. Charlemagne would rule for fourteen years before being succeeded by his son, Louis the Pious.

CORONATION COCKTAIL #1

1½ ounces sherry
1 ounce dry vermouth
¼ ounce maraschino liqueur
2 dashes orange bitters
Lemon twist

Add ice and water to a cocktail glass to chill the glass. Add ice to the mixing glass, then add sherry, dry vermouth, maraschino liqueur, and bitters. Stir at least forty times. Strain the contents of the shaker into the empty glass. Garnish with a lemon twist. Serve.

Louis XVI was nineteen years old when he acceded to the French throne in 1774. He aided the Americans in their revolution against Great Britain, for which the Americans honored him by naming Louisville, Kentucky, for him. However, a similar French uprising would see Louis XVI overthrown by his own people. After being tried, he was sentenced to death by guillotine.

GUILLOTINE

½ ounce butterscotch schnapps
½ ounce Irish cream liqueur
½ ounce peppermint schnapps

Prepare a shot glass. Pour the butterscotch schnapps in the shot glass. Using the back of a barspoon, layer the Irish cream liqueur and then the peppermint schnapps on top of the first layer to create three layers. Serve.

Henry IV and III, King of France and Navarre, respectively, was a serial philanderer. More than thirty women are recognized as his mistresses, and there were perhaps many more who have been lost to history. Henry came to the French throne as a Protestant in 1589. He eventually converted to Roman Catholicism, saying, "Paris is well worth a mass." Even though he escaped many assassination attempts, he was assassinated in 1610. After his death, he was known as Good King Henry because of his gentle manner and his concern for his subjects. He once said, "If God grant me life, I will see that every laboring man in my kingdom shall have his chicken to put in the pot."

ANGEROUS LIAISONS

1 ounce coffee liqueur
1 ounce Cointreau
½ ounce sweet and sour mix

Add ice and water to a cocktail glass to chill the glass. Add ice to the tin side of a Boston shaker. In the mixing glass, add coffee liqueur, Cointreau, and sweet and sour mix. Pour the contents of the mixing glass into the iced tin and secure the glass to the tin. Shake the contents until the ice sounds different and the contents are cold. Open the Boston shaker. Empty the cocktail glass, then strain the contents of the shaker into the empty glass. Serve.

Queen Sālote Tupou III was the longest-reigning monarch in the kingdom of Tonga and the first (and only) queen regnant. Sālote was crowned in 1918, reigning until she died in 1965. She is the grandmother of the current King 'Aho'eitu Tupou VI. Sālote is Tongan for Charlotte.

$\mathscr{Q}$UEEN CHARLOTTE

2 ounces red wine
1 ounce grenadine
4 ounces lemon-lime soda

Add ice to a Collins glass. Pour the red wine into the glass, followed by the grenadine. Top with the lemon-lime soda. Serve.

Simeon Saxe-Coburg-Gotha was the last Bulgarian monarch. He reigned as Tsar Simeon II from 1943 to 1946. As the communists took over Bulgaria, he moved to Spain and lived in exile until 1996, when the communists lost control of Bulgaria. In 2001, he was elected prime minister of Bulgaria, serving in that role until 2005.

SAR

1 ounce vodka
1 ounce Grand Marnier
½ ounce lime juice
3 ounces sparkling wine
Dash orange bitters

Add ice and water to a champagne flute to chill the glass. Add ice to the tin side of a Boston shaker. In the mixing glass, add vodka, Grand Marnier, lime juice, and orange bitters. Pour the contents of the mixing glass into the iced tin and secure the glass to the tin. Shake the contents until the ice sounds different and the contents are cold. Open the Boston shaker. Empty the champagne flute, then strain the contents of the shaker into the empty glass. Top the cocktail with sparkling wine. Serve.

Count Arnaud of New Orleans was known for drinking throughout the day: champagne and orange juice in the morning and later coffee with bourbon. This variation on a Rob Roy is named for the count himself.

COUNT ARNAUD'S SPECIAL COCKTAIL

2 ounces Scotch
1 ounce Dubonnet Rouge
3 dashes orange bitters
Orange twist

Add ice and water to a cocktail glass to chill the glass. Add ice to a mixing glass. Add Scotch, Dubonnet Rouge, and orange bitters. Stir the cocktail at least forty times. Empty the cocktail glass, then strain the contents of the mixing glass into the empty glass. Garnish with an orange twist. Serve.

King Alfonso XIII was the Spanish monarch from 1886 until 1931. Francisco Franco took over Spain in the late 1930s and ruled until his death in 1975. Alfonso spent most of the rest of his life in exile away from his kingdom. He would eventually be succeeded by his grandson, Juan Carlos I. His great-grandson Felipe VI is now king of Spain.

ROYAL HIGHBALL

4 ripe strawberries
1 ounce cognac
4 to 5 ounces sparkling wine

Add ice and water to a champagne flute to chill the glass. Muddle the strawberries in the bottom of a mixing glass. Add the cognac. Empty the champagne flute, then strain the contents of the mixing glass into the empty glass. Top the cocktail with sparkling wine. Serve.

When Prince Albert, Queen Victoria's prince consort, died at the age of forty-two in 1861, Great Britain fell into mourning. Consuming champagne was seen as disrespectful, so the Black Velvet was created: sparkling wine laced with stout to honor the late prince.

BLACK VELVET

2 ounces Guinness Stout
3 ounces sparkling wine
Lemon twist

Add ice and water to a champagne flute to chill the glass. Empty the champagne flute. Add Guinness Stout, then top the cocktail with sparkling wine. Garnish with a lemon twist. Serve.

The French kings traveled to the Reims Cathedral in the Champagne region to be crowned king of France. This cocktail is worthy of any royal or royal wannabe.

CHAMPAGNE COCKTAIL

3 dashes Peychaud's Bitters
3 dashes Angostura bitters
Sugar cube
1 ounce cognac
5 ounces sparkling wine
Lemon twist

Add ice and water to a champagne flute to chill the glass. Empty the champagne flute. Add the bitters, the sugar cube, and the cognac. Top the cocktail with sparkling wine and garnish with lemon twist. Serve.

As Prince of Wales, the future Edward VIII was visiting the United States during Prohibition. The prince visited a speakeasy owned by "Texas" Guinan. The establishment was raided. The quick-thinking Guinan put an apron and chef's toque on the prince and told him to cook eggs until the raid was over.

RINCE OF WALES

⅓ ounce simple syrup
Dash Angostura bitters
1½ ounces rye whiskey
Splash of maraschino liqueur
1 chunk fresh pineapple
1 ounce chilled sparkling wine
Lemon twist

Add ice and water to a champagne flute to chill the glass. Add ice to the tin side of a Boston shaker. In the mixing glass, add simple syrup, Angostura bitters, rye whiskey, maraschino liqueur, and pineapple chunk. Pour the contents of the mixing glass into the iced tin and secure the glass to the tin. Shake the contents until the ice sounds different and the contents are cold. Open the Boston shaker. Empty the champagne flute, then strain the contents of the shaker into the empty glass. Top the cocktail with sparkling wine and garnish with lemon twist. Serve.

Henry Beaufort was a member of the Royal House of Plantagenet and a bishop in the Roman Catholic Church. His father was John of Gaunt, Duke of Lancaster, and his mother was Katherine Swynford. In 1424, he performed the marriage ceremony of his niece, Joan Beaufort, and King James I of Scotland. Henry served as Lord Chancellor of England and was elevated to cardinal in 1426.

ISHOP

7 dried cloves
½ cinnamon stick
½ ounce honey
3 ounces boiling water
2½ ounces tawny port
½ ounce lemon juice
½ ounce orange juice

Add the cloves, cinnamon stick, honey, and boiling water to a mixing glass. Allow the mixture to steep. Strain into an Irish coffee mug. Add the port, lemon juice, and orange juice. Stir and serve.

The Archbishop of Canterbury crowns and anoints British monarchs. The last Archbishop of Canterbury to crown a monarch was Geoffrey Fisher, who was installed in 1945 and stepped away in 1961.

$\mathcal{A}$RCHBISHOP COCKTAIL

2 ounces gin
1 ounce green ginger wine
¼ ounce Green Chartreuse
Lime wedge

Add ice to an old-fashioned glass. Add the gin, green ginger wine, and Green Chartreuse. Stir, garnish with the lime wedge, and serve.

The Duke of Norfolk is the Earl Marshal or the person tasked with organizing the coronation of the monarch. The Howard family has held this title since 1483, when the title was created for John Howard, 1st Duke of Norfolk. Edward Fitzalan-Howard is the 18th Duke of Norfolk.

$\mathscr{D}$UKE OF NORFOLK PUNCH

1½ ounces brandy
½ ounce sherry
1 ounce milk
1 ounce simple syrup
Lemon twist
Orange twist

Add ice and water to a wineglass to chill the glass. Add ice to the tin side of a Boston shaker. In the mixing glass, add brandy, sherry, milk, and simple syrup. Pour the contents of the mixing glass into the iced tin and secure the glass to the tin. Shake the contents until the ice sounds different and the contents are cold. Open the Boston shaker. Empty the wineglass, then strain the contents of the shaker into the empty glass. Garnish with the orange and lemon twists. Serve.

The House of Romanov was the last ruling house of the Russian empire. Starting with Peter the Great in 1682 and ending with Nicholas II in 1917, the Romanov family enjoyed unchecked power over the land and people living in their domain. Today, descendants of the cadet lines of the imperial family argue over the rightful heir to the defunct throne.

$\mathcal{C}$HAMPAGNE ROMANOV FIZZ

6 strawberries
1 ice cube
2 ounces orange juice
2 ounces sparkling wine

Add ice and water to a champagne flute to chill the glass. Puree the strawberries, orange juice, and the ice cube together until smooth. Empty the champagne flute, then pour the puree into the empty glass. Top the cocktail with sparkling wine. Stir and serve.

The title Duke of Devonshire was created for William Cavendish in 1694. The current duke is Peregrine Cavendish, 12th Duke of Devonshire. The Cavendish family has connections with the Kennedy family in the United States and with the Spencer family in Great Britain.

$\mathcal{C}$AVENDISH

2 ounces vodka
2 dashes Angostura bitters
3 ounces sparkling wine
Lemon twist

Add ice and water to a champagne flute to chill the glass. Add ice to the tin side of a Boston shaker. In the mixing glass, add vodka and Angostura bitters. Pour the contents of the mixing glass into the iced tin and secure the glass to the tin.

Shake the contents until the ice sounds different and the contents are cold. Open the Boston shaker. Empty the champagne flute, then strain the contents of the shaker into the empty glass. Top the cocktail with sparkling wine. Garnish with a lemon twist. Serve.

The Kir Royale is a royal drink. The mixture of crème de cassis and champagne make for a wonderful cocktail.

IR ROYALE

½ ounce crème de cassis
5 ounces sparkling wine

Add ice and water to a champagne flute to chill the glass. Once chilled, empty the champagne flute. Add the crème de cassis, then top the cocktail with sparkling wine. Serve.

For those who need a little more kick in their cocktail, try the Martini Royale.

ARTINI ROYALE

2½ ounces vodka
½ ounce crème de cassis
2½ ounces sparkling wine
Lemon twist

*Add ice and water to a champagne flute to chill the glass.
Add ice to the tin side of a Boston shaker. In the mixing
glass, add vodka and crème de cassis. Pour the contents of
the mixing glass into the iced tin and secure the glass to the
tin. Shake the contents until the ice sounds different and the
contents are cold. Open the Boston shaker. Empty the champagne flute, then strain the contents of the shaker into the
empty glass. Top the cocktail with sparkling wine. Garnish
with a lemon twist. Serve.*

The British royal family enjoys the last name of Windsor by choice. Until recently, the lineage of the of family
was deeply German, up to and including the marriage of
Queen Elizabeth II and her consort, Prince Phillip, Duke
of Edinburgh. Starting with King George I and the House
of Hanover to Queen Victoria's marriage to Prince Albert
of Saxe-Coburg-Gotha to George V's marriage to Queen
Mary, the British royal family consistently married German
consorts. Technically, Queen Elizabeth's father, George VI,
would have been the last Saxe-Coburg-Gotha had his father,
George V, not changed the family name during World War I
from the German Saxe-Coburg-Gotha to Windsor. When
George V's cousin, Kaiser Wilhelm of Germany, heard the
news, he said he would look forward to the next performance
of the Shakespeare play *The Merry Wives of Saxe-Coburg-Gotha*.
George VI was the first British monarch since Queen Anne to
marry a consort with a non-German heritage.

INDSOR COCKTAIL

¼ ounce lemon juice
¼ ounce Cointreau
1 ounce applejack
4 to 5 ounces sparkling wine

Add ice and water to a champagne flute to chill the glass. Add ice to the tin side of a Boston shaker. In the mixing glass, add lemon juice, Cointreau, and applejack,. Pour the contents of the mixing glass into the iced tin and secure the glass to the tin. Shake the contents until the ice sounds different and the contents are cold. Open the Boston shaker. Empty the champagne flute, then strain the contents of the shaker into the empty glass. Top the cocktail with sparkling wine. Serve.

As with anyone in the public eye, royals live irregular lives because they are hounded by the press and the paparazzi. The simple things in life become monumental tasks. Royals go incognito!

NCOGNITO

1½ ounces vodka
1 ounce apricot brandy
4 ounces ginger beer

Add ice to a Collins glass to chill the glass. Add the vodka, brandy, and ginger beer to the glass. Gently stir and serve.

Another incognito recipe for those who need extra privacy.

$\mathscr{I}$NCOGNITO

2 ounces Lillet
1 ounce brandy
⅓ ounce apricot brandy
Dash of Angostura bitters

Add ice and water to a cocktail glass to chill the glass. Add ice to a mixing glass, then add the Lillet, brandy, apricot brandy, and Angostura bitters. Stir forty times. Empty the ice and water out of the glass and then strain the cocktail into the glass. Serve.

Recently, I visited Louisville, Kentucky. A former student recommended that I visit a new speakeasy on Washington Street named Hell or Highwater. As I reviewed their menu, the name of a cocktail caught my attention: the Common Wealth. At first, I thought the drink referred to Kentucky, but as I reviewed the description, I realized that the cocktail was a nod to the British Commonwealth.

The Common Wealth

1 ounce Redemption Rye
¾ ounce Marti Rum
½ ounce Cynar liqueur
½ ounce Bénédictine
¼ ounce Laphroaig Scotch Whisky
Dash Angostura bitters
Dash absinthe

Add ice and water to a cocktail glass to chill the glass. Add ice to a mixing glass, then add the rye, rum, Cynar liqueur, Bénédictine, Scotch, Angostura bitters, and absinthe. Stir forty times. Empty the ice and water out of the glass and then strain the cocktail into the glass. Serve.

BIBLIOGRAPHY

Amis, Kingsley. *Everyday Drinking*. New York: Bloomsbury, 2008.

Arthur, Stanley Clisby. *Famous New Orleans Drinks and How to Mix 'Em*. Gretna, LA: Pelican, 1937, 1944, 1965, 1972, 2013.

Buddemeyer, Ruby. "50 Strict Rules the Royal Family Has to Follow." *Marie Claire*, August 25, 2017.

Bullock, Tom. *The Ideal Bartender*. St. Louis: Buxton & Skinner Printing and Stationery, 1917.

Burke, Harman Burney. *Burke's Complete Cocktail & Drinking Recipes with Recipes for Food Bits for the Cocktail Hour*. New York: Books, 1936.

Crockett, Albert Stevens. *The Old Waldorf-Astoria Bar Book*. New York: A. S. Crockett, 1935.

Daly, Tim. *Daly's Bartenders' Encyclopedia*. Worchester, MA: Tim Daly, 1903.

Dick, Erma Biesel. *The Old House: Holiday & Party Cookbook*. New York: Cowles, 1969.

Duecy, Erica. *Storied Sips: Evocative Cocktails for Everyday Escapes, with 40 Recipes*. New York: Random House Reference, 2013.

Embury, David. *The Fine Art of Mixing Drinks: The Classic Guide to the Cocktail*. New York: Mud Puddle Books, 2008, 2009.

Fadiman, Clifton, ed. *The Little, Brown Book of Anecdotes*. Boston: Little, Brown, 1985.

Federle, Tim. *Tequila Mockingbird: Cocktails with a Literary Twist*. Philadelphia: Running Press, 2013.

Gilmore, Joe, and Nicholas Foulkes. *Joe Gilmore and His Cocktails*. N.p.: Sir David Davies, 2003.

Haigh, Ted, "AKA Dr. Cocktail." *Vintage Spirits and Forgotten Cocktails: From the Alamagoozlum to the Zombie and Beyond*. Beverly, MA: Quarry Books, 2009.

Hearn, Lafcadio. *La Cuisine Creole: A Collection of Culinary Recipes from Leading Chefs and Noted Creole Housewives, Who Have Made New Orleans Famous for its Cuisine*. New Orleans: Hansell & Brothers, 1885.

Hess, Robert. *The Essential Bartender's Pocket Guide: Truly Great Cocktail Recipes*. New York: Mud Puddle Books, 2009.

Jackson, Michael. *Michael Jackson's Bar & Cocktail Companion: The Connoisseur's Handbook*. Philadelphia: Running Press, 1994.

Johnson, Harry. *Harry Johnson's 1882 New and Improved Bartender's Manual and a Guide for Hotels and Restaurants*. Newark, NJ: Charles E. Graham, 1882, 1934, 2008.

Kappeler, George J. Modern. *American Drinks: How to Mix and Serve All Kinds of Cups and Drinks*. New York: Merriam, 1895, 2008.

Kosmas, Jason, and Dushan Zaric. *Speakeasy: Classic Cocktails Reimagined, From New York's Employees Only Bar*. Berkeley, CA: Ten Speed Press, 2010.

Leach, Alison, ed. *The Savoy Food and Drink Book*. Topsfield, MA: Salem House, 1988.

Lipinski, Bob, and Kathie Lipinski. *The Complete Beverage Dictionary*. 2nd ed. New York: Van Nostrand Reinhold, 1996.

Longford, Elizabeth, ed. *The Oxford Book of Royal Anecdotes*. Oxford: Oxford University Press, 1991.

Meehan, Jim. *The PDT Cocktail Book: The Complete Bartender's Guide from the Celebrated Speakeasy*. New York: Sterling Epicure, 2011.

Miller, Dalyn, and Larry Donavan. *The Daily Cocktail: 365 Intoxicating Drinks and the Outrageous Events That Inspired Them*. Gloucester, MA: Fair Winds, 2006.

New York Bartenders' Association. *Official Handbook and Guide*. New York: New York Bartenders' Association, 1895.

Pan, Jessica. "The 10 Most Bizarre Royal Etiquette Rules." The Cut: Royal Wedding 2.0, May 17, 2018.

Reed, Ben. *Ben Reed's Bartender's Guide*. New York: Ryland, Peters & Small, 2006.

Reekie, Jennie. *The London Ritz Book of Drinks: From Fine Wines and Fruit Punches to Cocktails and Canapes*. London: Ebury, 1990.

Rosenbaum, Stephanie. *The Art of Vintage Cocktails*. New York: Egg & Dart, 2013.

Schmid, Albert W. A. *How to Drink Like a Mobster: Prohibition Style Cocktails*. Bloomington, IN: Red Lighting Books, 2018.

———. *How to Drink Like a Rock Star*. Bloomington, IN: Red Lighting Books, 2020.

———. *How to Drink Like a Spy*. Bloomington, IN: Red Lighting Books, 2019.

———. *The Kentucky Bourbon Cookbook*. Lexington, KY: University Press of Kentucky, 2010.

———. *The Manhattan Cocktail: A Modern Guide to the Whiskey Classic*. Lexington, KY: University Press of Kentucky, 2015.

———. *The Old Fashioned: An Essential Guide to the Original Whiskey Cocktail*. Lexington, KY: University Press of Kentucky, 2013.

Stanforth, Deirdre. *The New Orleans Restaurant Cookbook: The Colorful History and Fabulous Cuisine of the Great Restaurants of New Orleans*. Garden City, NY: Doubleday, 1967.

Thomas, Jerry. *Bartenders Guide: Containing Receipts for Mixing*. 1887. Reprint. New York: Dick & Fitzgerald, 2008.

Tirado, Eddie. *Cocktails and Mixed Drinks*. London: Hamlyn, 1972.

Trader Vic. *Trader Vic's Bartender's Guide, Revised*. Garden City, NY: Doubleday, 1947, 1972.

Wellmann, Molly. *Handcrafted Cocktails: The Mixologist's Guide to Classic Drinks for Morning, Noon & Night*. Cincinnati, OH: Betterway Home, 2013.

Wondrich, David. *Imbibe!* New York: Perigee, 2007.

ALBERT W. A. SCHMID is a Gourmand Award winner and author of several books, including *The Old Fashioned: An Essential Guide to the Original Whiskey Cocktail*; *The Manhattan Cocktail: A Modern Guide to the Whiskey Classic*; *How to Drink Like a Mobster*; *How to Drink Like a Spy*; *How to Drink Like a Rockstar*; and *The Hot Brown: Louisville's Legendary Open-Faced Sandwich*.